TAIZÉ

'Ah, Taizé, that little springtime . . . . !'

JOHN XXIII

TAIZÉ

BROTHER ROGER AND HIS COMMUNITY

REX BRICO

COLLINS

Published by Collins
London · Glasgow
Cleveland · New York · Toronto
Sydney · Auckland · Johannesburg

The quotations from *Festival* and *Struggle and
Contemplation* by Brother Roger are reprinted
with permission of the publishers, SPCK,
London and The Seabury Press, New York.

First published in Great Britain 1978
UK ISBN 0 00 215824 8
© Rex Brico 1978
First published in the USA 1978
USA ISBN 0–529–05621–6
Library of Congress Catalog Card Number 78–59859
Made and printed in Great Britain 1978
William Collins Sons & Co. Ltd Glasgow

Contents

Illustrations

The photographs reproduced in this book are by the following photographers:

Pages 16–17, 26, 34–5, 43, 50, 59 top, 75, 82, 93, 99, 106, 114, 124, 131, 132, 138, 144, 156, 190, 212, 219
Hans Lachmann of Pressefoto Lachmann, Dusseldorf

Pages 10, 59 bottom, 60, 64, 150, 162, 170, 176, 184, 198–9, 204
Jacques Houzel of *La Vie*, Paris

Page 25 Fotografia Felici, Rome

Foreword

It is no easy task to write a documentary history of a community that, at the end of each calendar year, burns almost all of its documents. Such a practice may well illustrate the 'dynamic of the provisional' that characterizes Taizé; it doesn't make the journalist's job any easier. For that reason, the author of this book was led to rely to a great extent on the collaboration of the community for his information. For their abundant friendship he expresses his sincere thanks.

In the last decade Taizé has grown from a family of brothers (admittedly international and interconfessional) to an unparalleled point of attraction for young people from all parts of the world. This book deals with both: the monastic community and its friends. It is meant for all who are searching for an authentically Gospel-centred vision of life today, regardless of nationality, church affiliation, or age. One of the most important features of Taizé is the creation of a community beyond all inner and outer lines of separation.

Amsterdam, Christmas 1977   REX BRICO

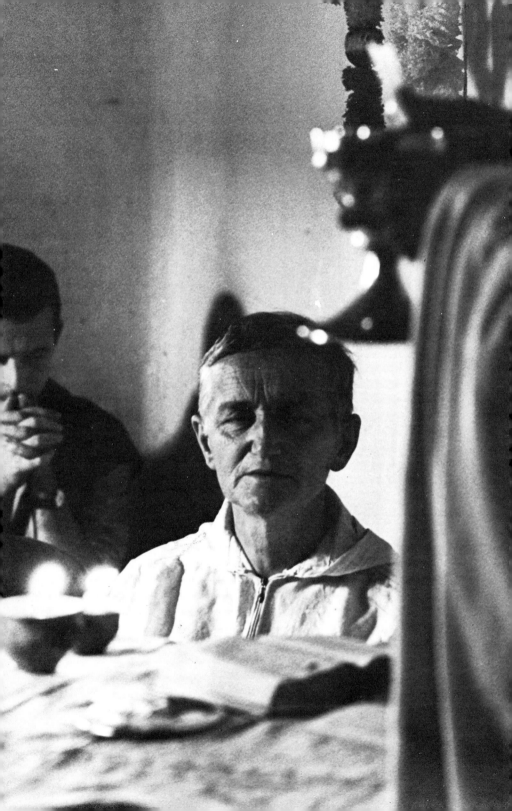

The Story of
a Mustard Seed

Most monastic orders owe their existence to one man or woman, and the Taizé Community is no exception. It would never have begun without the creative spirit and stubborn persistence of Roger Schutz. Anyone who knows him has no doubt that he can be ranked alongside Benedict, Bernard, Francis, Ignatius, Charles de Foucauld, and Mother Teresa of Calcutta.

The future Prior of Taizé was born on 12 May 1915 near Neuchâtel in Switzerland. An ordinary child, he was the youngest of a happy family of nine brothers and sisters. His father, a pastor from the Swiss Jura, gave a religious stamp to Roger's upbringing from the very beginning; his mother, of French stock from nearby Burgundy, prevented him from falling into a narrow nationalism. Roger recollects that from his early childhood he learned to look beyond denominational borders. From time to time his father used to go into a Catholic church to pray, certainly no common practice for a Swiss clergyman in those days. And when Roger reached the age of thirteen and lodgings had to be found for him near his school, his parents chose the family of a Catholic widow, who was poor and needed the money. As Brother Roger was to say later: 'I owe my ecumenical vocation to the generosity of my parents.' And he adds: 'I was surrounded by a living Catholic faith. There was no money in the house, they trusted in Providence and lived above all in the communion of saints. I might add that the family's devotion was by no means fossilized.' But Roger himself almost lost his faith in those adolescent years. The intolerant attitudes of both Protestants and Catholics were repugnant to him. 'That's why, as soon

Brother Roger taking communion

as I found my faith again, I looked for ways of living a vocation to Christian unity,' he says.

While he was still at school, Roger showed a keen interest in the monastic tradition. In addition to Pascal ('The heart has its reasons of which reason knows nothing') he was particularly interested in Port Royal, the birthplace of Jansenism. Later he understood why. 'An authentic monastic life, imbued with a spirit of renewal, contains within itself a unique power to accomplish a special vocation in the Church.' Neither Pascal nor Port Royal, however, brought his faith back. What did was a serious lung disease which kept him out of active life for a long time and gave him the opportunity to reflect in solitude. At twenty, he decided to study theology. 'It took an intervention of grace for me to see where God was leading me.' Nonetheless, it was obviously a difficult decision, as during his illness he had also begun to write. He produced a long essay entitled 'Evolution of a Puritan Boyhood', and considered a literary career. Full of hope, he offered the manuscript for publication in the *Nouvelle Revue Française*. But their answer, a request to re-write the conclusion, went against his conscience. He decided instead to study theology and spent four years at the universities of Lausanne and Strasbourg.

A decisive event in Roger's life occurred during his last year of studies, when he was elected president of the Protestant Student Federation in Lausanne. Inspired as he now was by the Christian message, he founded a group for the study of questions of faith in 1939. Out of this group grew a year later, under his leadership, a kind of 'third order', called the *Grande Communauté*. It was made up of twenty students, who through prayer and work attempted to help their Christian fellow-students out of their isolation and towards a common purpose in life. The *Grande Communauté* came together every other month for a colloquium, prepared by the members and other Protestant intellectuals. Like the retreats organized by the *Communauté*, the colloquia were characterized above all by an intense and authentic spirituality. 'Retreats are necessary,' wrote Roger, 'for much converse with God and little with his creatures.' They included meditation, examination of conscience, and confession. 'So that in the silence of a retreat a Christian is not left alone with the confusion of his own thoughts, another Christian accompanies him, remaining always at his side.'

Although the retreats attracted a great many people Roger regarded them as part of a larger perspective. And so in 1940 he decided to buy a house, a place where his group could pray and study while at the same time live in a region marked by human suffering. Such a region lay close at hand in unoccupied France, which was still controlled by the Vichy government. Not only had the war already caused great damage, but Jews, political refugees, and others no longer welcome in the part of France occupied by the Germans, came streaming into the region in an attempt to reach safety in neutral Switzerland. Often they had nothing but the clothes on their backs as they tramped from village to village, starving. And once they had reached Switzerland not everyone received them kindly, as is evident from a reading of the proceedings of the Swiss parliament in those years. A cabinet minister appealed to the 'justified egoism' of the Swiss people to take measures against this stream of refugees. Among Swiss students, however, were those who felt that something else was demanded of them. One of them took it upon himself to make a journey against the current.

So in August 1940, Roger travelled to Burgundy, where some of his mother's relatives were still living. After several days of searching for a house he found two excellent possibilities: one over the Swiss border near Geneva and another in the neighbourhood of Bourg. The first one included, in addition to a farm, a tiny chapel where Francis de Sales had once celebrated the Eucharist. The other stood at the foot of a hill and looked out over rich farmland. With his sense of spiritual beauty, Roger was enchanted by the possibilities. But he continued his journey, since he knew that was not why he had come to France. When he arrived in the town of Cluny, a lawyer drew his attention to the nearby village of Taizé, where a house large enough for his purposes had lain unoccupied for a long time. He rode out to it on his bicycle and found a tiny hamlet, half in ruins, almost completely abandoned by its inhabitants. In addition to the war, a series of bad harvests had turned the land into a desert. It was a hopeless, miserable sight. An old peasant woman, who kept the keys, showed him the house. When Roger asked where he could get something to eat she said, 'Here, with me'. During the meal she whispered, 'Buy the house and stay here! We're all alone!' And that tipped the scales. Roger now says: 'I chose Taizé because the woman was poor. Christ speaks through the poor and it's good to listen to them. Anyone who begins with the poorest of the poor is not likely to go wrong. Contact with them prevents faith from becoming vague and unreal.'

The rest of the group accepted Roger's decision to settle in Taizé, though they would have preferred a place in Switzerland. In September he bought the house through a lawyer in Cluny. Interestingly enough, on the very day he signed the deed, the impoverished owner of the house, Madame de Brie, was in Lyons ending a novena she was offering for its sale. A totally unexpected telegram brought her misery to an end.

In December 1940, after the necessary preparations, the *Grande Communauté* was able to hold its first meeting in their new quarters, which was called for the time being the House of Cluny. When the colloquium ended and the participants left, Roger stayed behind. Yet he was seldom alone. Living only a few miles from the demarcation line – the border between occupied territory and Vichy France – he was confronted almost hourly with refugees knocking at the door. Some arrived more dead than alive. Roger took them in and cared for them. He provided for himself and his guests by cultivating some of the adjoining land, and milking the only cow. Three times a day he retired for prayer and meditation to a room which he had turned into a chapel. In so doing he was extremely careful not to make his guests feel bound to join him out of gratitude. During this time he wrote an eighteen-page pamphlet, in which he briefly described his monastic ideal. Its main guidelines were: 'Every day let your work and rest be quickened by the Word of God; keep inner silence in all things and you will dwell in Christ; be filled with the spirit of the Beatitudes: joy, simplicity, and mercy.'

Although the house was searched several times and he received warnings from the Gestapo, Roger stayed on in Taizé until 1942. Then, one day in November, as he was helping someone across the Swiss border, news reached him that the German authorities had occupied the house and taken the refugees prisoner. It appears that one of the local inhabitants had denounced him. Roger accepted the consequences and remained in Switzerland. With Max Thurian, a theology student, and Pierre Souverain, from the Polytechnic Institute, two young men he had recently met thanks to the publication of his pamphlet, he rented a house in Geneva, in the shadow of the historic cathedral. There they were joined by a fourth, Daniel de Montmollin. Inspired by reading about Francis of Assisi, they committed themselves temporarily to celibacy and community of material goods, and every morning and evening they prayed together in a side chapel of the cathedral. In the meantime Max was preparing his dissertation on liturgy, and Roger his dissertation on 'The monastic ideal before Saint Benedict and its conformity to the Gospel'. To the question whether Christians could live a monastic life and still be faithful to the Gospel, he replied with an unequivocal yes which was certainly not wholeheartedly received in Protestant circles. Despite some resistance, Roger was able to defend his dissertation successfully and was ordained a pastor in 1943.

At first the group of four considered themselves part of the *Grande Communauté*, even its centre. But little by little the bonds between them weakened and Roger's group developed its own independent existence. The house of the four young men became a focal-point for all kinds of students, workers, and trades union officials. Much discussion went on; topics such as the right to own property, community of goods, and socialization of the means of production seemed to be most popular. Later a favourite subject was the catechism: at the request of the workers, the young men re-

15

Taizé

wrote it in simpler language. How strong the ties with working people were can be seen from the preface to Roger's first book, *Introduction to Community Life*, written by a group of metal workers. In it they state that at first they looked upon the Community of Cluny with some scepticism, but that they lost their suspicions when they discovered that there were Christians who wanted to share everything with one another. As early as 1941 Roger wrote: 'We are isolated from one another, and that breeds resignation. How can we make a break with our all-too-individualistic traditions? How can we make use of the immense possibilities which are liberated when people work together and live in community?' The rest of his life would answer that question.

Roger was not able to return to Taizé again with his three new brothers until near the end of the war in 1944. And they found that although many things had changed, few were improvements. The terror of the German occupation had been replaced by the hatred of the local French population for the German prisoners-of-war in a camp near the village. This hatred was so intense that one day some women entered the camp and murdered a young Catholic priest. The brothers of Taizé tried once again to foster reconciliation. They visited the prisoners and shared what little food they had with them; they even obtained permission to invite them occasionally to their house. And although several of the local farmers took offence, the brothers' forgiving spirit made an impact on many non-Christians in the area. Besides the prisoners, the brothers also took care of children who had lost their parents in the war, providing a home for them in the manor house at Taizé. The twenty children they took in were to find a mother in Geneviève Schutz, one of Roger's sisters.

In the meantime Brother Pierre, an agricultural expert, was doing wonders to improve the cultivation of the land around the house and by 1947 the community, which from the very beginning had supported itself entirely from the work of the brothers, was producing enough to be financially stable. They gave hospitality to a growing number of visitors: not only priests and monks, but also Protestant theologians and others who were curious to see at close quarters some 'twentieth-century monks'. The visitors were especially interested in the common prayer of the young brothers, which took place three times a day in one of the rooms of the house. Because of the guests who kept coming, the room was soon too small. To solve this problem the brothers asked the Roman Catholic Bishop of Autun for permission to use the little village church, a twelfth-century Romanesque chapel which had not been used for years. The request was granted, the reply coming from none other than the papal nuncio in Paris, Angelo Roncalli, the future Pope John XXIII. But a further request to the nuncio to allow an ecumenical meeting of monks and priests to take place at Taizé met with no response. Obviously the time was not yet ripe.

In 1948 three young Frenchmen – one of them a doctor – came and stayed with the group, so that by the beginning of 1949 the community numbered seven men. One question that kept coming up was whether their commitment should always be a provisional one. They concluded that this was holding them back and inhibiting new initiatives. That spring they crossed the Rubicon and at Easter all seven took the three traditional monastic vows. In the little Romanesque church, specially decorated for the occasion, they committed themselves for life to celibacy, community of goods, and the acceptance of an authority, represented by the figure of the prior, Roger. The event went almost unnoticed by the world outside, even though it marked the first time that the centuries-old monastic ideal had become a reality in the Churches of the Reformation. In the words of Brother Roger: 'We always tried not to let ourselves be influenced by the experiences of others. We wanted to start completely afresh and experience everything all over again. In spite of this it became evident to us one day that we could not remain faithful to our vocation without committing ourselves to community of goods, acceptance of authority, and celibacy.'

Now that the Community of Taizé had become a reality, ecumenical contacts with the Churches could more easily be undertaken. In that same year Brothers Roger and Max journeyed to Rome to meet Pope Pius XII and other Church officials. They pleaded for closer relationships between the Churches, but for the moment they met a wall of stubborn resistance. Pope Pius did not appear to want to do much to promote ecumenism; he seemed somewhat afraid of it. This became evident in 1950 when he promulgated a dogma concerning Mary which to all appearances widened the gap between Rome and the Reformation Churches. Many Protestants began to doubt whether an ecumenical discussion with Rome was possible at all. Spirits fell, but in Taizé the courage to go on won the day. In 1950 Brothers Roger and Max took a second trip to Rome, this time for meetings with Monsignors Ottaviani and Montini (the future Pope Paul VI) in addition to the Pope. This time they were promised that the Vatican would send fully accredited auditors to the ecumenical conference of Faith and Order, a commission of the World Council of Churches, to be held in 1952 in Lund, Sweden.

The early fifties saw other milestones in the history of the community. From the time that the first seven brothers took their permanent vows, their numbers increased steadily. They soon decided that they could not restrict their work and ministry to the immediate region, and decided to send two of their number to live at Montceau-les-Mines, forty kilometres north of Taizé, to work in the mines. It was their intention that they should be 'signs of Christ's presence and bringers of joy' among the workers. As they did in Taizé, the two brothers stopped for prayer three times a day; they attempted as well through the trade unions to help the mine workers' struggle for their rights. As a result of their action very soon no factory in the region would take on any of the brothers from Taizé, but that did not stop them: Montceau became the first of an impressive series of 'fraternities', always provisional, begun in places of material or spiritual poverty. Usually such fraternities are composed of between two and four brothers, who support themselves as far as possible. Since Montceau-les-Mines, the Taizé Community has had fraternities in Abidjan, Amersfoort, Bad Boll, Beirut, Calcutta, Chicago, Chittagong (Bangladesh), Coventry, Davao City (Philippines), Geneva, Hussein-Dey (Algeria), Kigali (Rwanda), Keulen, Lyons, Madison, Marseilles, Mont Beliard, New York, Niamey (Nigeria), Paris, Recife (Brazil), Rome, Santiago, Sheffield, Utrecht, Västerås (Sweden), Villigst, and Vitória (Brazil). Brothers have worked as male nurses in war-torn Algeria, dock workers in Marseilles, and welfare workers among ghetto residents in Chicago. In 1977 a new style was inaugurated, an 'itinerant fraternity' composed of two brothers who went to Cameroon and who, instead of settling in one place, kept moving throughout the country, visiting one local church after another in the style of the early Christians. Other brothers were preparing to leave for an extended stay in the United States. All the fraternities keep in regular contact with the prior.

In the winter of 1952-3 Brother Roger wrote out the Rule of Taizé in detail. Unlike most traditional monastic rules, it was inspired by an experiment in community living which had already been going on for some years: a number of brothers had already been living its chief principles for some time. The Rule does not lay down the hours of prayer or details of this kind, nor does it tell the brothers what they should wear. Instead it attempts to suggest a spirit and to motivate and inspire a way of life. It often does this by quoting phrases from the Bible; this may be taken as an illustration of the fact that the first brothers were well grounded in Scripture. 'There is a danger in having indicated with this rule only the essentials for a common life,' says the Rule. 'Better to run that risk, and not settle into complacency and routine. . . . That Christ may grow in me, I must know my own weakness and that of my brothers. For them I will become all things to all, and even give my life, for Christ's sake and the Gospel's.'

With the election of John XXIII to the See of Peter, a new phase began in Taizé's relationship with the Roman Catholic Church. Immediately after his election in 1958, the new Pope received the French cardinal Pierre Gerlier, who had become a good friend of Taizé. The aged cardinal urged the Pope to pay special attention to the ecumenical movement, still in its youth, and asked him to receive Brother Roger of the Taizé Community as a gesture in this direction. Despite his many appointments at the time of his coronation, Pope John promised to see him soon, 'provided the questions are not too difficult'. Brother Roger was summoned to Rome and greeted a few days later by the Pope with the words, 'Ah, Taizé, that little springtime . . . !' Years later Brother Roger explained what the meeting meant to them. 'That audience,' he recalls, 'gave a new stimulus to our ecumenical endeavours. From then on Pope John had an unexpected influence on us and, without knowing it, let a little springtime be born for Taizé.' The visit was repeated annually, and the practice continued later with Pope Paul VI. The Roman Catholic attitude towards Taizé changed significantly in those years, and when the Second Vatican Council began in 1962, Brother Roger and another brother were asked to be present at the sessions as guests. During their stay they set up a fraternity of five brothers in a little flat near the Roman Forum. Day after day they welcomed Council fathers for prayer and a meal. Their guests included both Roman Catholic and Orthodox bishops as well as Protestant Church leaders. Council debates and documents were often the topic of conversation, and it would be no exaggeration to say that many texts showed the influence of these talks. In this Roman apartment a close friendship was formed with the Chilean bishop Manuel Larrain and other South American prelates, such as Bishop Santos and Dom Helder Camara. Before Bishop Larrain left Rome (he was to die shortly afterwards in an automobile accident), he gave Brother Roger his episcopal ring as a token of the bond between them. Out of these Latin American visits to the fraternity grew among other things Operation Hope, a campaign launched by the community to provide financial help to small co-operatives of Latin American peasants and fishermen. Operation Hope did not receive its final form in Rome, however, but in the recently completed Church of Reconciliation in Taizé. In 1960 talks were held in Taizé between Roman Catholic bishops and pastors from different Protestant traditions. Since this was the first ecumenical discussion at that level with the Catholic Church since the Reformation, it created so much publicity that the number of visitors to Taizé immediately increased. In 1960 it became clear to the brothers that the village church was far too small to hold them *and* their guests. It took time to find a solution, however, since funds to build a new church were simply not at hand. And then 'Aktion Sühnezeichen', a German movement begun after the war to undertake projects as signs of reconciliation in areas where the German occupation had wrought havoc, took charge of the initiative. The Germans found both the funds and the volunteers to erect the building. One of the brothers drew up the plans and on 6 August 1962, the Feast of the Transfiguration, the dedication ceremonies took place. Numerous Church dignitaries were present for the occasion: Bishop Martin of Rouen represented the Catholic Church; Metropolitan Meliton was present in the name of the Patriarch of Constantinople; Bishop Tomkins came as the special envoy of the Archbishop of Canterbury; Bishop Scharf as presiding bishop of the Synod of the German Protestant Church; and the Reverend Marc Boegner as president of the Federation of Protestant Churches of France. The World Council of Churches was represented by the majority of its Central Committee, then in Paris for their annual meeting. Together the brothers and their guests created an ecumenical event quite unique in the history of the Christian Churches. On the evening of the dedication Brother Roger declared: 'Consciously or not, people who come to Taizé are in search of something beyond themselves. When they ask for bread, how can we offer them stones to look at? When they have been in the Church of Re-

conciliation, it is better for them to remember the call to reconciliation and, with this as a basis, to prepare the daily bread of their
lives, rather than to return home with only the memory of stones.'
The answer depended upon the Churches, but not all ecclesiastical associations or organizations were ready to react posi-
tively to such a call. So, for example, in the Geneva headquarters
of the World Council of Churches, the complaint was heard repeatedly that Taizé had no business to set itself up as an ecumenical
arbitrator. Dr Visser 't Hooft, founder and head of the World
Council, felt that this role should be reserved for official institutions in Rome and Geneva, and he made no bones about his
opinion. Relations with the World Council improved greatly in
1966 when Visser 't Hooft was succeeded by the American Dr
Eugene Carson Blake. Even before he assumed his duties, Dr
Blake visited the community and expressed his deep appreciation
of the work of the brothers. From then on he was a regular visitor
to Taizé. In 1968 he invited Brother Roger to speak at the World
Council Assembly in Uppsala, and the following year he asked the
community to collaborate in the work of SODEPAX, the joint commission for peace and justice of the Vatican and the World
Council of Churches. Carson Blake's successor, Dr Philip Potter,
was later to visit Taizé on countless occasions, and became regarded as a warm and faithful friend. Visits to Taizé by Church
leaders too numerous to mention continued throughout the following years; one such visit of particular importance occurred in 1973
when Dr Michael Ramsey, then Archbishop of Canterbury, was
welcomed by the community for a short stay.

It was the dedication of the Church of Reconciliation in 1962,
rather than any other event, that brought Taizé out of the obscurity
of its previous existence. Newspapers all over the world wrote
articles, magazines took pictures and camera crews came to film.
Above all else the daily prayer of the brothers, now held almost exclusively in the large church, captured people's interest. It aroused
astonishment in Catholic circles, where the traditional Latin
liturgy was falling out of favour. In Reformation circles it was re-

Brother Roger with (above) Pope John XXIII in 1963,
and Pope Paul VI in 1968

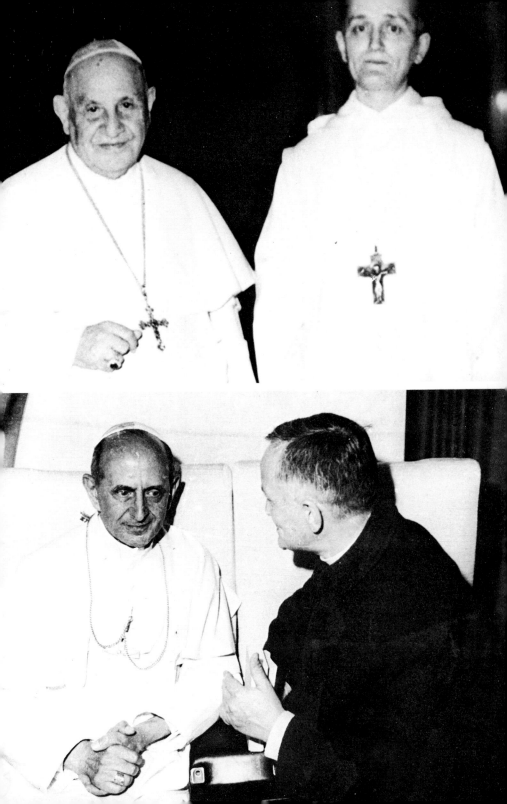

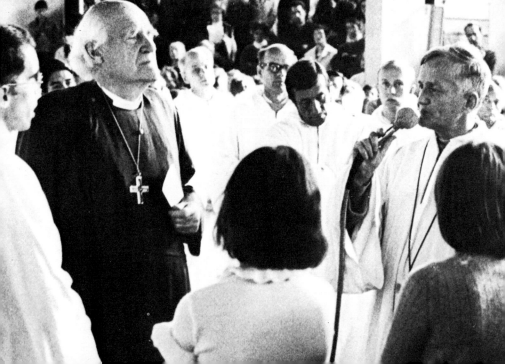

garded with mixed feelings. Protestants suffering from the lack of formal liturgical celebrations in their tradition applauded the common prayer of Taizé. Other Protestants saw it as confirming what they had feared all along, from the beginning of the community's existence: that Rome was infiltrating the Reformation Churches through the back door. In any event this did not diminish people's curiosity, and the number of visitors continued to increase. Interest was so great that in 1965 the community decided to build a guest-house near the Church of Reconciliation. It was erected on a shooting-range which the village council of nearby Cormatin leased to the brothers. The guest-house was named 'El Abiodh', after the village in the Sahara where Charles de Foucauld had lived. Later two new wings were added, 'Constantinople' and 'Lambarene'.

By the mid-sixties relations with neighbouring villages such as Cormatin seemed far better than they had been during the community's early years, and this could be partly explained by the way in which the brothers had been working their land. Already in the fifties they had noticed that local farmers felt themselves unequal to the more efficient agricultural methods of the brothers, made possible on account of their greater expertise. In addition, all kinds of historically rooted, often inexplicable, prejudices had to be taken into account. Indeed, the centuries-old dechristianization of Cluny and its environs may have been due in no small part to the economic pressures once exercised by the renowned Benedictine abbey. From the start Taizé was extremely careful not to confirm anti-monastic prejudices. When in 1954 a local factory, in an attempt to lower prices, threatened to stop purchasing from the farmers in the area, the community joined with a number of them to form a dairy co-operative, which today collects, processes, and sells the milk of more than 1200 producers. This co-operation built up trust and in 1962 the COPEX was born, an agricultural co-operative, still in existence, in which the community and some of the local farmers pool their resources and share profits accordingly. Finally, in 1965, the brothers decided to give all the community's

27

Cardinal Bea visited Taizé in 1966 (above)
and the Archbishop of Canterbury, Dr Ramsey, in 1974

land to the COPEX, except for the plot of ground on which their house and the surrounding buildings stood. The recently published encyclical of Pope John XXIII, *Mater et Magistra*, undoubtedly had a lot to do with this decision, as did Brother Roger's meeting with a number of Latin American bishops who had recently shared out among poor peasants a great deal of the property belonging to their dioceses. In Rome the prior stated: 'We have chosen this kind of co-operation because we are convinced that community of goods is not only important for us, but also for lay people. . . . Our common life does not dispense us from the necessity of earning our daily bread. On the contrary, it is our duty not only to support ourselves by our own labour, but likewise to support others and in this way to take a very concrete part in the *œcumene*, which means the community of people throughout the earth.'

Both the gift of land and the reasons for it shed much light on the manner in which the prior and his brothers wished to see the Gospel take root in the life of society. This was only to be expected after the choice of Taizé as a place to live and after the discussions in the house in Geneva. For anyone with a knowledge of the history of the community, it is simply a matter of becoming more and more consistent with a vision which was there from the outset.

The younger generation remembered this in 1968, after the student revolts which had erupted in Paris petered out in frustration. When the students, after the hesitant and ambiguous reactions on the part of the authorities, seemed to have no place to go with their beleaguered ideals, only one place still remained where older people seemed to understand them: Taizé. There people had already been working for years to change structures – antiquated Church structures, hard as rock, but, in the immediate surroundings, the structures of society as well. Thousands of students descended upon Taizé, both Christians and non-believers, young men and women of every possible background and viewpoint. Between the periods of common prayer they talked to their hearts' content. Like it or not, for the outside world at least, Taizé had added a political dimension to its image: Taizé was *engagé*.

By 1969 the community had become so ecumenical as regards Churches that it counted brothers from the Reformed, Lutheran, and Anglican traditions among its number. That Easter it took a further significant step in that direction when a young Roman Catholic doctor from Belgium joined the community. Other Roman Catholics, including priests, followed. Cardinal Marty, Archbishop of Paris, gave his approval. To mark this new development the brothers drew up a text at their yearly council which said among other things: 'The mere presence of Catholic brothers among us stimulates us to live more and more an anticipation of unity by feeling ourselves united with that minister who is the servant of the servants of God.' The declaration prepared the way, so to speak, for later statements by Brother Roger regarding the papacy. In it the prior said that every community, and therefore also the universal Church, needs a pastor to foster unity and communion among all, but he added that this pastor could not ask non-Catholics to deny their fathers. Denying is the opposite of loving. Brother Roger: 'Why should he (the Pope) not pronounce "Catholic" men and women who are living a faith that is truly universal and ecumenical, while at the same time not expecting them to give up the evangelical values their traditions have transmitted to them? He alone has at his disposal the power to declare that all who confess one and the same essential faith are "of the Church". With "the violence of peace-makers", we dare to ask for such an act of courage.'

With the entry of Catholic priests into the community, inevitably problems of Church discipline arose. The most difficult was undoubtedly the celebration of the Eucharist, which Rome considered (and still considers) an expression of and not a means to unity. While waiting for a breakthrough in this area, Taizé found a working solution which attempted as far as possible to respect all the different points of view: Roman Catholic and non-Catholic priests celebrated Mass and the Lord's Supper respectively in dif-

29

ferent chapels in the crypt of the Church of Reconciliation. The elements consecrated at the Catholic Mass were reserved and distributed near the icon of the Virgin Mary in the church, those from the Lord's Supper near the icon of the Cross by the altar. Brother Roger, though an ordained pastor, does not celebrate the Eucharist any longer, thus questioning by a personal gesture this state of affairs.

The year 1969 was in other respects a turning-point in the history of Taizé. The number of young people visiting the hill had become so great that many in the traditional Churches began asking themselves what it was that was attracting so many young Christians to that hill in Burgundy. Surprisingly, of all the topics proposed for the group discussions, ecumenism appeared to attract the least interest. And it seemed that one week of searching together with others for the essential in one's life was no longer sufficient. The meetings were in danger of becoming sterile owing to the lack of continuity with people's daily lives. And so the question arose as to what ways could people find of keeping in touch after leaving Taizé and of going forward together in quest of a renewed Church. Brother Roger discussed this with a small group of young visitors to Taizé in February 1969. It was off-season, yet people from forty-two different countries were present! Spontaneously Brother Roger thought, 'We are like a council of youth'. That autumn, it was decided that everyone would go home with a few questions, to be answered by each person in his or her own situation: What are we really searching for? What will enable the whole of Christ's Church to free itself from the blind alley of its divisions? What joyful news do we, the young, have to offer the People of God? In his journal Brother Roger noted: 'For months past, one thing has been preoccupying me: with the present discord in the Church, what act could give peace to those who are shaken and strength to those who are committed? I sense that such an act should be a gathering of an exacting nature, regularly repeated for the years to come.

Over a certain period of time, building and searching together. And with that, again and again the same thought dominates: this demanding gathering is going to be a council of youth. But who will carry it out? As far as we are concerned, there is no comparison between the effort needed and our possibilities.'

A few weeks before Easter 1970 a team of young people from every continent gathered together in Taizé to evaluate the results of seven months of searching. They included a peasant from the north-east of Brazil, an immigrant worker from Portugal, a resident of Chicago's black ghetto. Together they decided to transmit some 'joyful news'. 'We have been attentive to the suggestions of youth from all five continents. We have grasped the fact that for a very large number, there exists a thirst for God but, at the same time, the will to move forward in the service of mankind. For them, it is all or nothing. . . . What we have understood most clearly is that people are waiting for a quite new and different project that will commit them totally for Christ, which sets free their energies and which will prepare within them an outburst of creativity so that the world may be made fit to live in. Then, the violence of hatred can still be changed into the "violence of the peace-maker". . . . Young Latin Americans have felt "the urgent necessity for a Church which is more and more paschal, which refuses every means of power, and is a faithful witness to a Gospel which sets men free" (Medellin Conference, 1968). Africans and Asians find themselves turned away by the Northern hemisphere from the values of communion, sharing, and festival which are theirs.' 'For the Christian,' wrote Justine from Zaire, 'festival is the certainty that Christ has taken our human feasts and raised them to the level of his Risen Life. The Christian festival is wholly compatible with suffering and struggle. The Christian who is deeply committed to life always has an inner hope. Living the festival means living the joyous anticipation of Christ's return.'

'In our search for a way to answer their hope,' continued the intercontinental team, 'at a time when the Church is going through a desert, and when the earth is becoming uninhabitable for many, we called to mind the first Christians. At the beginning "they held everything in common, they were of one heart and mind," and their brotherly unity could be seen'. The team too wanted to transmit a festival of communion, and so the 'joyful news' came into being, a short text read on Easter Day 1970 to the young people gathered together in Taizé.

That day they represented the largest crowd the hill had yet known: 2500 young men and women from thirty-five different countries. The weather was not in their favour: strong winds, rain, and even snow drove them out of their tents, and they were forced to look for shelter in nearby villages, in the Church of Reconciliation, the reception house, and even in the rooms of some of the brothers. But this stroke of bad luck did not dampen their spirits, as was clear when morning prayer was over and brothers distributed hot chocolate and agape rolls in front of the church. Guitars appeared from nowhere; singing and dancing began! *Le Christ est ressuscité !* – 'Christ is risen!' Later, during the evening prayer, the 'joyful news' was read out. A member of the intercontinental team took the microphone and said: 'The Risen Christ comes to quicken a festival in the innermost heart of man. He is preparing for us a springtime of the Church: a Church devoid of means of power, ready to share with all, a place of visible communion for all humanity. He is going to give us enough imagination and courage to open up a way of reconciliation. He is going to prepare us to give our lives so that man be no longer victim of man.' And then Brother Roger announced: 'We are going to hold a council of youth.'

The reactions of the young people tightly packed in the church defied description: at first there was a tense silence while they digested the news, then clapping turned into deafening applause, foot-stamping and shouting, which died away to return again with a noise like thunder. Several minutes later Brother Roger continued: 'This council will be composed of a majority of young people, but in order to avoid all segregation, older people, elderly people, and even children will take part. The council will be a long march through the desert, setting out without knowing our destination.'

Why a council? Because 'when the very first Christians found themselves faced with a question without a solution, when they were on the point of dividing, they decided to gather in council', as the First Letter to the People of God was to express it four years later. But this argument did not convince everyone. Some clerical voices were opposed to the word 'council', feeling that it had to be reserved for official ecclesiastical institutions. Others were frightened by the emotion unleashed by the joyful news. The spontaneous behaviour of those who came to Taizé did not fit the image of the Church in which most of the critics had grown up. But leaders of the Churches reacted favourably. Pope Paul VI declared that he was following the events in Taizé with attention and sympathy, a message he was to repeat in greater detail at Epiphany 1971, and again later on. Dr Eugene Carson Blake, Secretary General of the World Council of Churches, published an open letter to the brothers and the young people, in which he expressed his appreciation of the efforts of Taizé 'to break through the present impasse of ecumenism'.

And so, it was decided to hold a Council of Youth. But what exactly would it include? Thick dossiers? Seven-day conferences? Voting? Amendments? Resolutions? None of all that. So what then? Nobody really knew, not even the prior. No detailed, theoretical plans were in existence, at most there was a shared intuition. This meant that the Council had to become an adventure proceeding the other way round from the great historic councils. They consisted of bishops meeting together to make decisions, which then were put into practice at the ground level of the Church. Taizé decided instead to begin by living new forms of Christian communion, and to talk about it – in Taizé or elsewhere – only later. Those forms were always created in the tension between two fundamental poles: struggle and contemplation. To put it another way: young people, wherever they happened to be, found each

other both in common prayer and in shared concern for the oppressed, the exploited, the lonely, and the hopeless. In this combination lay the new life by which they wanted to make the Church of Christ credible. Brother Roger wrote: 'When faced with the fact that very many young people reject the Church, why stand still to interpret that pessimistically, anxiously, or even polemically? Is not the main thing to question ourselves thoroughly so as to discern beyond the immediate event the signs – already visible – of a springtime of the Church?'

So Easter 1970 was the starting-point for the long desert march which the Council was to become. Young people who had met one another on a deeper level at Taizé remained in touch when they returned home. Each one started out from his or her own situation, from a Church group, a Third World action group, or even a trade union. People came together regularly, visited one another, or met in Taizé. Others left for distant lands, in order to strengthen existing contacts and to form new ones. Young people from Brazil, France, and Cameroon travelled through Belgium and Luxembourg; a boy from Sri Lanka and two from France visited Australasia; an Indian travelled through the United States. There was even more correspondence by letter. To handle this flood of letters, the community had to open its own post office. Slowly a common awareness of a new life-style began to grow, for which Taizé served as a sounding-board, the antenna to gather news of what was springing up here and there. From time to time a new intercontinental team of young people in Taizé went through the letters and other reports. In that way in the days before Easter 1971 a new message took shape. It attempted to answer the question: what are the consequences of the festival announced a year ago? The team answered: 'It implies a struggle to let all take part in that same liberating festival. . . . Becoming aware of oppressions. Committing our energies to breaking with situations where man is victim of man. Rejecting privileges. Refusing the hunt for success. Furthering communion among all. Finding liberation – our own, and our neighbour's both near and far away. Being released ourselves so as to secure others' release.' How? 'So that the news may pass from one to another, so that little by little it may bring back to life all that is inert among Christians. We are still situated in the hidden, underground movement of the Church. We are being led to live incognito, like leaven hidden in the dough, like seed buried in the ground, seeking poverty of heart, always using poor means, without gold or silver.'

When this and other messages were read out at Easter 1971, the Church of Reconciliation seemed too small to hold the thousands of people present. The problem was solved drastically and unconventionally: the façade of the building was knocked down and a circus tent set up in its place. The reason was that Christians live the dynamic of the provisional. The People of God are constantly on the move. The gesture was prophetic, too, since the following Easter the number of visitors more than doubled. Preparations for the Council had by that time become so intense that Brother Roger was able to announce the opening for 1974. The intercontinental team announced that the two years to come would require much imagination: 'They will also be two years of courage, during which we shall be trying to hasten towards man's tomorrow, towards a technological civilization with enormous potential for the promotion of the whole of mankind. However, we shall not hesitate, when necessary, to become signs of contradiction, when profit and consumer values become dominant.'

During Holy Week and Easter 1972 it already seemed as if a council were taking place at Taizé. A few days earlier five hundred young people of different nationalities had arrived to welcome the sixteen thousand visitors from more than eighty countries. They were subdivided into groups of a hundred, which in turn were divided into fluid cell-groups of ten. It was an attempt to work against the feeling of being part of an anonymous mass. One evening sixty different meetings took place in and among the brightly coloured tents on the hill. At all hours of the day and night you could find young people in the Church of Reconciliation and its crypt deep in prayer. During the day priests

37

and brothers were always present in the church for personal conversations.

The Eucharist on Easter Day was celebrated by a young priest from Togo, in the presence of the Archbishop of Vienna, Cardinal Franz Koenig, and World Council Secretary, Dr Eugene Carson Blake. Messages were read from the Pope and the Patriarch of Constantinople. Those were only two of the hundreds of telegrams which came in from around the globe, mostly from young people involved in preparing for the Council. Those who could not be present for this celebration were an important part of the meetings nevertheless. First of all by being mentioned in the impressive liturgy, which fired the enthusiasm of the participants. But also in the drawing up of the interim balance-sheet. The contours of the Council began to take on a somewhat clearer shape. It did not aim at creating a new organization or Church, but a new way of thinking; not a reform of Christian life or of the Church, but nothing less than a rebirth. That was why the Council of Youth began with an 'inner adventure', involving personal prayer and a deepening of life in Christ. An inner adventure that was not intended merely in an individualistic sense.

During the early seventies 'grass-roots communities' inspired by the announcement of the Council of Youth sprang up in great numbers, not only in Europe, but also in South America and elsewhere in the Third World. In general such groups were made up of about seven people, who came together for common prayer at least three times a week, but who tried to live each day in the spirit of the Beatitudes – joy, simplicity, and mercy. They were kept together by an 'animator', who remained in touch with Taizé, and they were asked to be willing to break with every situation in which human beings are victimized by others, even to the point of giving their lives. Of course this meant different things in different countries. Imitating Taizé was to be avoided, since in very different situations that would quickly lead to caricature. That was also the reason why these groups would soon be integrated as far as possible into the life of the local Church and society. 'Try, rather, to be creative from your own starting-point,' wrote Brother Roger. 'Taizé is only the name of one small family. It is better not to use the name of Taizé too much.'

Young people made visits to others in practically every country in the world. 'We do not want to reach a springtime of the Church without having given the largest number of people possible the opportunity of working for it,' was the motto. So-called 'listening posts' were set up in Dakar (Senegal), Kigali (Rwanda), Bogotá (Colombia), Recife (Brazil), Bombay (India) and elsewhere, since 'we want to listen above all to the very poor, and that means the Southern hemisphere. For so long we have made that part of the world an economic – and even a spiritual – by-product of the North.'

In the course of 1972 it seemed necessary to discover what was really important for the growing number of pilgrims on their long march through the desert. To find out how the countless young people, linked in mind and in heart to the Taizé Community, were experiencing the Council preparations and how they envisaged the Council itself. For this reason a list of questions was drawn up and published in the *Letter from Taizé*, the (as it was then) quarterly news-letter published in ten different languages, including English, and sent to some 100,000 people in 130 countries. The questions were: How, concretely, do you envisage the Council? What life-style can be imagined for those not afraid to become signs of contradiction? What are the means of being (alone, in cells or in communities) bearers of the festival of the Risen Christ? How can we help find a new face for the Church? What really new acts of courage can be imagined so that man be no longer victim of man? Thanks to the replies, which flowed in from all parts of the world over the following months, the brothers and the intercontinental team were able to sketch the main lines of the coming Council at Easter 1973. It would be opened with a celebration in Taizé from 30 August to 1 September 1974, and be followed by celebrations in Latin America, North America, Asia, and Africa. The first year of the Council would thus be a year of mobility.

In the meantime, however, the intercontinental team proposed to the 18,000 young people meeting in Taizé at Easter 1973 that the coming stage of the preparations be devoted to 'struggle and contemplation to become men and women of communion': 'Any seeker of communion with God and with man is at once seized by the tension: struggle and contemplation. Two attitudes that seemed to contradict or oppose each other, and finally one is found to lie at the heart of the other, one begetting the other in a ceaseless exchange. Struggle within ourselves, to be freed from interior prisons and from the desire to imprison others. And struggle in company with the poor, so that their voice may be heard and systems of oppression smashed. Contemplation, so that little by little our way of looking can be transformed until we consider man and the universe with the eyes of Christ himself.'

This emphasis on struggle and contemplation by the intercontinental team was, incidentally, nothing new for Taizé. Already in the forties, it will be remembered, the brothers' day-to-day work consisted of caring for refugees and prisoners in need alongside times of prayer and meditation. Despite the bustle of preparing for the Council, this spirit was preserved intact, and shone through in 1973 in the striving for communion with Jesus as well as with the poor, oppressed, and exploited all over the world. In Taizé, then, there were no false contradictions between struggle and contemplation, between piety and social commitment, between horizontalism and verticalism, or whatever names you care to give to the prophetic and mystical dimensions of life. The one inseparably linked to the other, as if that were the most ordinary thing in the world. And this, against the background of a Christianity which at that very moment, in the early seventies, was being torn apart by polarization and heresy-hunting. 'In the darkest hour of the night, the experience of the Resurrection is born for me when I see the neighbourhood communities reliving the age of Peter and Paul, in prayer vigils for their brothers in prison,' a young Latin American wrote to Taizé. 'Who is in a more sub-human situation: the Southern world, or the Northern?' asked two of his fellow-countrymen. 'Is happiness really a matter of living in a developed technological civilization, in a society of luxury, with buying, owning, comfort, and individualism as the basis ? . . . It is not possible to love God, who cannot be seen, if we do not love our neighbour whom we can see.' And a boy from Africa: 'May all the young people in the world learn that the evil from which we suffer comes from the same virus: profit, conquest, domination, self-centred appropriation. . . .'

At Easter 1974 all the fundamental ideas which had come up and been announced over the past four years were once again discussed and evaluated. During this last stage everyone was asked to answer one question: Given what you have already discovered and lived in the preparation of the Council of Youth, what are the elements that you would want to see contained in the Council itself? The answers would bring to light what had grown up in those years. Without straining after effects, the inner adventure, in all its depth and breadth, would have to be brought out into the open. But not as a bureaucratic movement with the usual structures of hierarchical organizations and channelled responsibilities, but like a river that widens as it flows, like a fabric growing before your eyes. In Asia one would say: like a lotus gradually opening. With the aim of helping the People of God to be renewed in its very being, totally committed in struggle and contemplation; to make the Church once again a people that celebrates the Resurrection of Christ, a poor people, with no means of power, a place of communion for all. That is why, the young people wrote, it is not important how many will take part in the Council of Youth. Often even a small number of men and women, ready to risk all, hoping against hope, have been able to change the course of events.

It is worthy of note that here too the Taizé Community was ahead of the young people. Between 1970 and 1974 the brothers risked a reputation they had worked hard to build up in the course of thirty years – a fragile reputation of reconciliation and self-denial, based upon respect for historical traditions and cultural individuality. And all the time there was the risk that the Council of

Youth would turn out to be nothing but a laughing-stock and destroy all the goodwill that had painstakingly been built up. But the brothers took that chance and it seemed to lead to positive results – for the moment, at any rate: after Easter 1970 Taizé welcomed 20,000 visitors; during 1971, 35,000; in 1972, 50,000; in 1973, 70,000; and during the year the Council opened, more than 100,000. And the very quality of these visits seemed to validate the risk the brothers had taken. Three times each day practically all the young people present came together to pray: workers from Milan, students from the Sorbonne, seminarians from the Congo, a peasant from Argentina. Among them were Catholics, Protestants, Eastern Orthodox, agnostics, even atheists. Times of prayer alternated with discussions about the Church, society, communism, what the Council would turn out to be, how to meditate, and many other topics. In the evenings people sang *Laudate Domino* around a camp-fire, accompanied by guitars and crickets. Particular interest was shown in the zones of silence arranged for reflection. Because an adventure without reflection is not a Christian adventure.

'In the four and a half years before the Council,' one of the members of the intercontinental team wrote, 'the preparation brought together many of us who were striving to build a world of justice and to place Christ at the centre of our lives. In each meeting or visit a dialogue was begun in which we joined one another beyond the usual stereotypes and separations which restrict and limit people. Each Easter, one particular aspect of the "joyful news" was chosen to be explored during the year. So the opening of the Council in the summer of 1974 was based not only on the material preparations which we were making, but on all that had been lived and felt during the four and a half years.'

Finally, as a sort of crowning touch to the preparations, it seemed that those four and a half years had made others think, not only young people. In 1974 Brother Roger was awarded the Templeton Prize and the German Publishers' and Booksellers' Peace Prize. The Templeton Prize is a kind of Nobel Prize for

religion, awarded by representatives of the great world religions to individuals who have helped others grow in the knowledge and love of God. In 1973 the Templeton Prize went to Mother Teresa of Calcutta. Brother Roger received the German Peace Prize because 'together with his brothers, men from all the Christian Churches, he has created a living example of ecumenism. He shows young people from an immense variety of backgrounds, beliefs, and ideologies a way out of their seemingly hopeless existence to life with a meaning. He passionately proclaims the "violence of peace-makers" and, in a ruthless age, courageously shows the way towards a more human future.' In past years, this prize had been awarded to Albert Schweitzer, Romano Guardini, Paul Tillich, and President Senghor of Senegal, among others.

When, on 10 April 1974, Brother Roger received the Templeton Prize, he stated in the London Guildhall that he 'would go to the ends of the earth, if necessary, to speak over and over again of my confidence in the new generations, my confidence in the young'. At the reception of the German Peace Prize, on 13 October of that same year in the Pauluskirche of Frankfurt, he said in part: 'As I try to understand everything in today's young people, I discover, behind so many different expressions, a passionate search to communicate. For Christians this communication becomes communion. The young of today desire it with the greatest possible number of mentalities and races. Many of the young have realized that being in communion with the misery of the world means also sharing in the world's struggle to overcome its misery.'

The opening of the Council of Youth on Friday, 30 August 1974, made a new and unconventional kind of Church history, not least by the fact that the long-awaited and thoroughly prepared event brought more than 40,000 people from practically every country in the world to a tiny village hitherto virtually unknown. The opening ceremonies lasted three days and in the months that followed were described in the most enthusiastic terms. One of the most factual was a story by an American journalist, Geneva Butz, mimeographed on an inconspicuous sheet that quickly became yellowed with age and forgotten. In her article, Ms Butz described how she arrived two weeks before the opening with other groups at Taizé to help with the preparations. Every day hundreds of young people arrived, some by train or car, others hitchhiking or even on foot. Everyone was immediately welcomed and put to work. One group transformed entire fields into camping-grounds, others built roads, others formed reception teams, an entire international orchestra, first-aid teams, groups to assist the press and the television people who were swarming around, and so forth. When the evening of the thirtieth arrived, the 40,000 had been settled in tents covering the greater part of the hill. The evening prayer celebration began with a 'Prayer for the Whole World', a long universal intercession for the needs of those farthest away (Korea, Japan), those suffering most (Vietnam, Bangladesh, Palestine, Sahel, Chile, certain Eastern European countries), and the most neglected minorities (North and South American Indians, Australian Aborigines). There was then a Scripture reading followed by an intense, meditative silence which, more than anything else, brought people together. Church leaders read messages: Cardinal Jan Willebrands on behalf of the Pope, Dr Philip Potter for the World Council of Churches, and others on behalf of the Patriarch of Constantinople and the Archbishop of Canterbury. Conspicuous among the scarlet cardinals, purple-mantled bishops and black-frocked Protestant Church leaders on the podium was the tiny figure of an elderly member of the Roncalli family, the brother of the late Pope John XXIII. Finally all eyes were directed towards the white-clad figure of Brother Roger, who took the microphone and said: 'The day has come, this opening day of the Council of Youth, the day when we all long to say: open yourself to understand each person fully, every woman and man, made of the same stuff as you and who, like you, searches, struggles, creates, prays. . . .' The opening service was closed with a hymn and the Our Father.

45

After the service the crowd returned to the tents and, about midnight, they learned for themselves that Burgundy can be swept by almost tropical rainstorms. A torrent deluged down upon the canvas roofs, the wind rose and the temperature dropped drastically. Many had to flee their waterlogged tents and look for dry quarters in the Church of Reconciliation. By the time the Saturday celebration came around, the landscape had turned into one big mud puddle. Nobody could escape it. While people waded through the thick morass to the six circus tents which had become a makeshift cathedral, a percussion ensemble played a composition entitled 'Struggle and Contemplation' . . .

During the midday prayer, twelve young people spoke of the sufferings in their respective lands. Gabriel from Bangladesh spoke of his Church abandoning young Christians in his country in their struggle for justice; Henriette from Senegal said that there the earth was thirsty and the barns empty, and their last goat had been taken for taxes; John from Philadelphia talked of the fear of the faceless ones, the anonymous figures who make decisions behind closed doors. An expression of the same reality was given liturgically by a procession of the Cross, making its way slowly through the crowd. At the end of the service, Brother Roger announced that soon he would be going to Chile 'to listen, to pray, to seek to understand, with the trust of love, both the poor and those in whom I admire the total gift of their lives'. The applause went on and on. Finally a youth said: 'Here among us there are others who would be taking too great a risk were they to speak, to say nothing of those who are not able to leave their country to be with us here. In communion with all of them we shall now stay in silence.'

The third celebration, on Saturday, was perhaps the most impressive. Interspersed with the reading of the Beatitudes in different languages, nine young people told of the signs of hope already visible in their respective situations. Interrupted from time to time by applause, they spoke of improvements in the ways people relate to one another, the new situation in Portugal, a growing social and political awareness among peasants in Latin

America. After some Scripture readings, candlelight spread out quickly from the centre of the crowds to fill with light the farthest corner of the six gigantic circus tents, arranged like the petals of a flower. Everyone held in his hand a candle, lit by his neighbour. The sea of light gave a dimension of irrefutability to the massive, many-voiced alleluias which echoed through the canvas cathedral. In order that the harsh realities of life should not be forgotten, however, the liturgy was immediately followed by a vigil of silent prayer in the Church of Reconciliation. Thousands of young people filled the church until the early hours of the morning, kneeling or sitting on the ground, united in mind with the countless people reduced to silence in prisons, in persecuted communities, or in dead-end personal situations. Meanwhile priests and brothers were distributing the consecrated elements to all who wished to receive Communion.

The climax of the three days of celebration came with the Sunday morning service. The theme 'Kindle a Fire on the Earth' was translated into a personal challenge for everyone by means of a 'Letter to the People of God', read aloud by Joseph from Zaire. In the months and years to come, young people throughout the world would find in it important topics for discussion and guidelines for action. It is a powerful letter, composed by the intercontinental team and Brother Roger on the basis of letters and discussions which had taken place beforehand. 'We have been born into a world which for most people is not a place to live in,' it begins. 'A large part of mankind is exploited by a minority enjoying intolerable privileges. Many police states exist to protect the powerful. Multinational companies impose their own laws. Profit and money rule. Those in power almost never pay attention to those who are voiceless.' The question is asked: 'What way of liberation are the People of God opening?' The letter answers that in the course of four and a half years young people have crossed the world in every direction and that, because of this, gradually a common awareness has emerged. It has been more particularly shaped by the voices of those who are living under subjection and oppression, or who are reduced to silence. Numerous Churches, states the letter, in the Southern as well as the Northern hemisphere, are being watched and even persecuted too. 'Some of them show that without any bonds with political powers, without means of power, the Church can experience a new birth, can become a force of liberation for humanity and can radiate God.' Another part of the People of God compromises with the prevailing inequality. 'Christians as individuals and many Church institutions,' says the letter, 'have capitalized their goods, accumulating vast wealth in money, land, buildings, investments. . . . Church institutions acquire highly efficient means of accomplishing their mission. . . . But many discover that gradually life vanishes, leaving the institution to turn over empty. . . . What they say is losing its credibility.' The letter points to the first Christians, who were known for their sharing, prayer, and simplicity. It then asks the Church: 'What do you say of your future? Are you going to surrender your privileges, stop capitalizing? Are you at least going to become a "universal community of sharing"? . . . Are you going to become the "People of the Beatitudes", having no security other than Christ, a people poor, contemplative, creating peace, bearing joy and a liberating festival for mankind, ready even to be persecuted for justice?' If we are actively involved in this, concludes the letter, we know that we cannot demand anything exacting of others unless we ourselves stake everything. We shall dare to live the Council of Youth as an anticipation of all that we want.

After the Letter to the People of God had been read, Brother Roger quoted part of a letter he had written with the title *Vivre l'Inespéré* ('Living Beyond Every Hope'), which he addressed to each one of the young people personally to help them 'fashion [their] lives in communion with Christ who is love'. Before the Sunday service ended, young people took candles to the four corners of the tents as a sign that the Church, faithful to her vocation, is called to kindle a light everywhere in the world. Finally Brother Roger addressed himself to an old woman, the mother of Polish resistance fighters, and to Giuseppe Roncalli, brother of the late

Pope John XXIII, who made it possible for many to leap over the wall of doubt concerning the Church. 'It is perhaps partly because of that very old man, John XXIII, that we are gathered here today. Yes, we have nothing to fear, we shall live something unexpected. How? No one can tell. We shall live a springtime of the Church and the voice of the poor will be heard . . .'

In this way all the celebrations of the opening of the Council of Youth made the same connections: between struggle and contemplation, belief and politics, prayer and social commitment. What the young and the brothers were clearly aiming at was wholeness of life, an attitude and a mentality that not only strives for communion among all Christians (and ultimately all human beings), but also for inner communion between God and the world. A task no one can accomplish alone. 'What can we do on our own?' Brother Roger asked rhetorically. 'With the whole People of God, collectively, it is possible to light a fire on the earth.' So the Council would have to be celebrated across the entire earth. Young people in every country would have to give concrete form to the Letter to the People of God starting from their local situations. For some the accent would lie on an analysis of social structures, on an unwavering effort to change relationships in society, while others would find in it inspiration to give up excessive prosperity and privileges, to visit old people, to share their possessions. Thus every celebration would be under the sign both of the universal Christ and of local needs.

As early as December 1974 the first Council celebration took place outside of Taizé, in Guadalajara, Mexico. The *colonia* Santa Cecilia was chosen as the most suitable place, a district of about 30,000 inhabitants, primarily families of masons, factory workers, unemployed persons, and displaced farmers. Most were illiterate and living far below the poverty line. To find lodging with these families, in their poor, tiny houses, for a few thousand young people from all over Mexico and South America, seemed an al-

most impossible task. Nevertheless they succeeded, and afterwards the guests were unanimous in saying that they would not have wanted to miss living in and with the families, that it allowed them to see at close hand the 'rebirth of the Church among the very poor'. 'Sharing with those who do not speak out, but whose whole life is one unbroken cry,' as a woman journalist expressed it.

The Mexican celebration was prepared during the whole month of December by having prayer three times a day in specific places. Visits were made to many of the fifty grass-roots communities which the district contained. These communities are in the habit of meeting once a week to reflect upon their problems in the light of the Gospel. Many of the local residents, adults included, took part in the celebration itself, which lasted three days. The participants were divided into six groups, which met for discussions, often out in the open. The liturgical celebrations, in which all participated, were held in the local parish church. They culminated in a solemn high Mass, a series of accounts by young people of oppression and hope, and an impressive candlelight procession. At the end the conviction was strongly expressed that the continuation of the Council of Youth in Latin America would depend to a large degree on the grass-roots communities existing there. But in view of the positive attitude of these communities regarding the celebration in the *colonia* Santa Cecilia, a certain optimism seemed justified. Brother Roger, who was present for the festivities, said later, 'Among the inhabitants of Santa Cecilia I glimpsed with my own eyes a foreshadowing of that Church which God is preparing for us in places where people are poorest'.

Council celebrations also took place among the poor of Latin America during January–February 1975 in Goya, Argentina, and Vitória, Brazil. In Goya, the poor farmers are among the most exploited and oppressed people; through their dependence upon the rich land-owners they are deprived of basic human rights. This became clear during the celebration when members of the Agrarian League of Corrientes described the desperate struggles of the farmers to keep their heads above water and assure a better life for their children. Such accounts alternated with discussions, music, theatre, and dancing, after which the celebration came to an end with a pilgrimage by the Christians of Goya to the chapel of the Holy Virgin of Itati. At least five hundred young peasants, workers, and students from all over Argentina took part in the event. In Vitória, where the Taizé Community had a fraternity, the celebration was held for the most part in a large wooden barn set amidst shacks without electricity, running water, or sanitation. Here as well, young workers and peasants told stories of suffering and of hope for a more human existence. The week before, prayer vigils had been held in different churches, and during the celebration an 'Assembly of the People of God' was staged, at which no less than 10,000 people, young and old, took part. Together with the local bishops, they marched in a long procession to the stadium to signify that the Church is always on the move. The grass-roots communities made sure that the 1200 participants from elsewhere in Brazil, Paraguay and Chile found lodgings with the inhabitants of Vitória. 'From South America, I saw the Council of Youth as a slight breeze bearing along a few seeds of communion,' noted Brother Roger that year. 'A breeze carries, without being visible in itself. The Council of Youth is not visible as something distinct. . . . Every communion is fragile. In the Council of Youth this is bound to be so, since we have no intention of acquiring followers, we have no system to defend, or a cause which must triumph. Christ himself was a man without defence. Christ does not ask us to defend ourselves, but to abandon ourselves.'

During his journey through Latin America in the beginning of 1975, the prior of Taizé was especially impressed by the disinterested way in which a growing number of bishops, priests, and lay people were committing themselves for a Church preaching not only contemplation but also struggle, justice, and liberation. In Chile he was particularly struck by the work of the so-called 'Committee for Peace', an ecumenical organism founded after the coup d'état to aid the persecuted, prisoners, and the families of those in prison, executed, or missing. In mid-November when the

Chilean government ordered this committee to disband, Brother Roger immediately sent a telegram to Cardinal Silva Henriquez of Santiago, in which he wrote: 'Following my voyage to Chile, I kept silent. Today I must speak out in the face of the suppression of the Committee for Peace by the Chilean government. In Santiago, I saw with my own eyes the work accomplished with unflagging courage by this committee, to give aid to the most unfortunate and hope to those in despair. I have confidence in your powers of discernment to discover ways of continuing this work. With so many others in Chile, you are a living witness of the Risen Christ in agony until the end of the world. Rest assured of my faithful support.' (The Cardinal found ways of continuing, by setting up a short time later a vicariate to handle this work.)

It was hardly surprising in the light of the Latin American celebrations that the Council of Youth in North America was opened, in March 1975, in a black neighbourhood in the heart of Philadelphia, a ghetto of ruined and abandoned houses and streets littered with garbage. Humanly a dead end, the home of broken and wounded lives, it was also a place where a small group of white Americans and Europeans had settled some years before simply to pray three times a day, to open lines of communication, and to try and break through the existing barriers of incomprehension and mistrust. Very slowly they succeeded, and the ghetto opened to the world. A small congregation became, for a week, a place of reconciliation for Americans of different backgrounds, as well as for young people from fifteen other countries. They prayed and sang, discussed and meditated. 'There where all seemed lost,' wrote a participant later, 'the promise of the Beatitudes is being fulfilled. For those with eyes to see this handful of Christians provides us with a vision of the springtime of the Church, a Church whose only security lies in Christ.' From this church a number of different visits were made, and so the Council spread to a Spanish-speaking neighbourhood in New Jersey, a 'ghetto' of abandoned old people in Manhattan, a centre for work with drug addicts. The celebration came to an end with a weekend in Hicksville, a suburb of New York City.

Easter 1975 once again brought 18,000 guests to Taizé, among whom were 3000 Spaniards. Both at Easter and on the 'Day of the People of God' held on 17 August, new announcements or themes were absent; the content and the consequences of the 'Letter to the People of God' and 'Living Beyond Every Hope' were still the centre of attention. Joseph from Zaire summed up the reigning mood when he said, 'On our own, we cannot do very much. But by the Council of Youth, we discover that the Church is a people. A people on the move. A people able to offer signs of hope – often very hidden, but already alive.'

But in 1975 the emphasis was on the American continent. After Philadelphia, a celebration took place in early May in Alabama. The site was a 'quilting bee', a women's sewing co-operative which was, according to the young organizers of the celebration, a sign of hope among the poor black farmers and sharecroppers of the region. For the celebration, a corner of the building where the women worked was decorated with products of the co-operative and turned into a makeshift chapel.

That same month, a Canadian celebration in Lachute, Quebec, was held in a place of pilgrimage staffed by Franciscan brothers. Among the more than one thousand participants were groups from Taizé, Philadelphia, Guadalajara, and Alabama. Their presence strengthened the image of the Council of Youth as a fabric woven between different countries and continents. As a symbol of this, everyone taking part was given a thread to place on a loom at the entrance of the church during a night of prayer. The multi-coloured fabric which resulted was hung over the altar for the Sunday Eucharist. This celebration showed how such different cultures as that of French and English-speaking Canadians could be interwoven: by celebrating the liturgy together, by discussing common programmes of action, and simply by living together for a few days. After she returned home, one of the participants wrote to the person who had been her host during the meeting: 'I came to

55

your house, but it was not just your house that I found, because you were there, my brother from Quebec. You welcomed me; you shared your sufferings, your life, your struggle, and your hope with me. I understood this, and I tried to do the same. And now we walk together in the joy that arises from struggle and contemplation, you here, me far away in Mexico, each with his own people, each following the steps of the Risen Christ, who awakens festival in us, who is the music of our festival.'

For the fifth Assembly of the World Council of Churches, held in November 1975 in Nairobi, Kenya, invitations went to two brothers of Taizé. They joined approximately two thousand Church leaders, observers, guests, journalists, and World Council staff members for three weeks of talks, conferences, and discussions in the gigantic, ultra-modern Kenyatta Centre. Almost all of the delegates stayed in the luxurious, Western-style hotels which crowd the centre of Nairobi. But not the two Taizé brothers. A few months before the 'most significant meeting in the history of ecumenism' began, a group of young people – from England, France, Indonesia, and Cameroon – had already rented a small house in a poor outlying district of the city, close to one of the worst slums in Africa. The brothers found a place to stay nearby in the home of a young Muslim.

As a Russian Orthodox bishop was later to remark, the brothers and the young people radiated the authentic spirit of the first Christians. During the day, while the brothers were present at the ecumenical conference, the boy from Cameroon worked in a training-centre for unemployed young men, one of the two girls helped in the slum, the Indonesian boy worked with a priest who took homeless children off the streets and cared for them. Another girl remained at home to welcome neighbours and guests. They all prayed together in the evening, usually with a hundred or so other people. Most of them were Church delegates – synod leaders, bishops, and other prelates – but a number of the local residents were present as well. After the service they ate soup, mixed freely with one another, and sometimes went on talking till late at night.

Since their house could only hold about twenty-five people, the tiny courtyard in front was used as well.

Anyone who did not experience this simple Christian presence – so contrary in style to the Assembly, which had cost millions – can hardly imagine what it was like. The nearby slums, which house about 80,000 people who have come from the countryside, have neither running water, sewers, electricity, nor streets. An ankle-deep layer of mud covers the ground, and there is a reek of urine. The 'houses' are made of wooden planks, pieces of cardboard, rags, and corrugated iron. On average there are fifteen people to a shack, which is generally no larger than the average living-room in the Western world. A kind of home-made liquor is distilled to help people forget their misery and their hunger. Many of the men desert their families, women often turn to prostitution, and children roam about with no roof over their heads and no food to eat. The priest with whom the Indonesian boy was working tried to find sheds where such children could sleep and eat. During the weeks of the Assembly, at least, he did not feel he was alone, thanks to the help of the Taizé group and the support of the many others who kept in contact with them.

From Kenya the brothers went on to Cameroon, where the first African celebration of the Council of Youth was held in Douala at the end of December 1975. The celebration was preceded by a series of meetings in different sections of the city, which keeps on growing as people flow in from the countryside. For a week guests from other countries and other regions of Cameroon shared the life of families there and the activities of Catholic and Protestant parishes, including the Christmas celebration with its traditional dances and songs. Every day they met with neighbourhood groups, young people working in parishes, teaching religion, involved in different movements. These meetings, held in a shed turned into a chapel, often went on by the light of an oil lamp until late at night. They brought together the People of God in all its diversity: once-warring ethnic groups, street vendors, students, workers, those out of work. The meetings culminated in three days of common prayer alternating with reflections in small groups on a number of topics. One text which was used seemed to have been written especially for the occasion . . . by the bishops of Chile!

While still other celebrations of the Council of Youth were taking place in Lubumbashi (Zaire), Pueblo (Mexico), and Melbourne (Australia), in Taizé Brother Roger and an intercontinental team indicated, on the eve of Easter 1976, what the next stage of the Council would be. About 15,000 young people from at least eighty different countries crowded on to the hill. When they had pitched their tents and were gathered all together in the Church of Reconciliation, enlarged with circus tents, they found a new challenge set before them: the radicalism of the paschal commitment.

The idea of a paschal commitment as such came from Spain, but the desire for a more concrete involvement had been expressed everywhere over the previous months. The whole evolution of the Council of Youth was leading towards this Gospel radicalism. And so, at Easter, Brother Roger and the young people produced a document in which they stated that a 'conciliar stream' had come into existence, spreading out and flowing towards other seekers of communion. 'Everywhere are manifest the same thirst for God and the same cry for justice,' said the text. 'Still, a large number of people in the world are without hope of any kind. Their future is closed. . . . How to pierce the walls of indifference and hopelessness ? . . . A long time ago, Christians started to take or renew a lifelong commitment during the night of Easter. So are we too going to say yes to a Gospel radicalism, to a paschal commitment ?' The paschal commitment: 'Certain that a small number of women and men, spread across the face of the earth, striving to reconcile in themselves struggle and contemplation, can change the course of history and reinvent the world: because of the Risen Christ, are you going to risk your life day after day, constantly setting out anew, never discouraged because loved with Eternity's love ? Will you let yourself be consumed by the passion for a communion in Christ's wounded body ? With the whole of God's people, will you open up paths of hope for all the human family ?'

Brother Roger with Cardinal Kim of Korea at Taizé (above) and with Mother Teresa and the author in Calcutta, 1976

Along with the paschal commitment it was announced that some young people would go on long journeys. Between the opening of the Council and Easter 1976 many thousands of young people had visited Taizé, but for many others who were interested, especially in the Third World, means were lacking. Brother Roger announced that at the end of the year he would go to India and Bangladesh, together with an international group of young people, to write a 'Second Letter to the People of God' there. 'All winter, here at Taizé we had many discussions with young Asians,' stated the prior. 'And it is true too that we have brothers living in Bangladesh. They experience conditions not fit for human beings, sharing the life of the very poor. Through these brothers of ours it is as if our very own flesh were entering into the poorest of peoples. From the exchanges of this winter has come the conviction of new risks which have to be taken.'

One of these risks would be that in Calcutta, the prior and the young people would work in Mother Teresa's Homes for the Dying. To get to know her better and to live a certain reciprocity, Mother Teresa would come to Taizé during the month of August. With Brother Roger she wrote a prayer that was later used regularly in the Church of Reconciliation and elsewhere in the world. It runs: 'O God, the Father of everybody: you ask all of us to bring love where the poor are humiliated, joy where the Church is downcast and reconciliation where people are divided – the father with his son, the mother with her daughter, the husband with his wife, the believer with whoever cannot believe, the Christian with his unwanted fellow-Christian. You open this way for us so that the wounded body of Jesus Christ, your Church, be leaven of communion for the poor of the earth and in the whole human family.'

The departure for India and Bangladesh announced at Easter took place in late October from Germany, where meetings had been organized in Tübingen and Münster beforehand. Those meetings, on the eve of the journey to the Third World, were not by chance: just as the wealthy inhabitants of postwar Germany contrast strongly with their suffering fellow-Christians in Southern

Asia, so the economic status of many young Germans clashes with their growing desire for a new life-style, for deep communion. The thorough preparations for the two meetings aimed at answering the question: 'How can we discover hope in a situation where there seems no possibility for change?' The meetings themselves helped answer that question, being visible signs of hope. People could hardly remember when the cathedral of Münster had ever been so full; some 10,000 young people from all over Germany came together for the occasion. Long before the evening prayer began, young people and old, Germans and foreigners from far and near, were already sitting packed together on blankets on the floor. The Protestant church in Tübingen could not even hold all the people, and so Brother Roger's address had to be transmitted to a neighbouring church. 'As time goes by, I realize more and more that as my life wanes I am being called to say how capable the young are of reinventing the world,' said the prior in his speech. 'That is why, in the coming years, I shall go to the far ends of the earth, to its uttermost bounds, to speak over and over again of my confidence in the younger generations.' The addresses were part of unforgettable celebrations, in which thousands sang music arranged for several voices and where Bible readings alternated with prayers and times of silence. Mention was made of suffering prisoners, those oppressed and exiled, the ill and the unemployed, foreign workers and all those who find no love on their way through life.

The day after the celebrations Brother Roger left for Bombay, where he was present as one of his brothers was ordained a priest. Then he travelled to Chittagong in Bangladesh to visit Taizé's fraternity there. Shortly before, in September, the first Council of Youth celebration in Asia had taken place in Bangladesh. The celebration was the longest to date: for two weeks some 350 students, workers, and other young people from Bangladesh lived as a community with the local population. For five days, they prayed and discussed fundamental questions of faith in a student hostel; then for a week they visited parishes and youth groups in remote villages, in blistering heat alternating with torrential rains; finally in Chittagong they celebrated together with young Hindus, Muslims, and Buddhists. Bishops from different Churches participated in parts of the celebration, which included frank discussions, dramatic performances, and frugal meals. A young Bengali active in a Church aid organization later summed up his impressions in this way: 'During the Council of Youth celebration it became clear to me that for years we have been thinking too much about projects and too little about people, who are really the important thing. The Council of Youth pointed out a new direction to me: first discover yourself in order to be able to liberate others. I have found confidence again. Now I am going to live and work with a group of young people in a poor Hindu village. I am going to risk everything to help those young people discover the power slumbering in them. . . .'

After his visit to Bangladesh Brother Roger returned during the month of November to India, where he joined the other brothers and the young members of the intercontinental team. In the meantime they had found a place to live in Calcutta, where they would write the Second Letter to the People of God. How they found the place was typical: for weeks they wore out the soles of their shoes walking through poor districts of Calcutta in search of a suitable location. Although clergymen had offered rectories and other church buildings – attractively located, surrounded by grass and trees – the brothers and the young felt it would be in contradiction to the purpose and spirit of their visit. Finally they met an Indian family with eight children, living in a house on Bedford Lane, an alley in a poor slum. Bedford Lane is characteristic of the living conditions of the majority of the Indian people, particularly the inhabitants of Calcutta: at the entrance to the alley you find a huge pile of garbage, where famished dogs, chickens, cockroaches, and other insects swarm. In this neighbourhood an average family earns less than $10 a month. But because of sickness, death, and unemployment, many families have to get along with no steady income at all. Since social security is unknown, a man without work

63

must turn to begging to survive; girls and women are forced into prostitution in the better parts of town. This generous family put a part of their house at the disposal of the Taizé group – three dilapidated rooms and a garage. The whole group lived there: five brothers and ten young people from England, the United States, France, Spain, Germany, Austria, Zaire, India, Argentina, Brazil, Indonesia, and the Philippines. For five weeks they worked, ate, prayed, and slept on the hard floor. For the length of their stay in India the group followed a fixed daily schedule. Morning prayer at six thirty, followed by a Eucharist. The rest of the morning was spent working in some of the homes of Mother Teresa and other social institutions: Homes for the Dying, homes for lepers, abandoned children, and clinics. After the midday prayer, afternoons were spent sitting in a large circle on the floor to work together on the letter. The evening prayer, at seven o'clock, often drew a crowd, warmly welcomed by the group. In this predominantly Muslim neighbourhood many of the local children came, as well as sisters and brothers of the Missionaries of Charity, and young and old from other parts of the city. There one could meet the Cardinal Archbishop of Calcutta, who celebrated Mass one evening in front of the house, the Anglican Bishop of Calcutta, Mother Teresa, a Dutch social worker from Bihar, and various student chaplains. Many stayed after prayer to share the simple meal, mostly of rice and curry, tea and bananas. Crowds of children, many of whom had no parents and led a wandering existence, were ever-present.

The Second Letter to the People of God, the result of the stay in Calcutta, was read on Sunday, 5 December in Notre Dame of Paris. Once again, the reader was the young drama student Joseph Ndundu from Zaire. Along with more than 10,000 people from almost every European country, those present included Brother Roger and a group of brothers, Cardinals Marty of Paris and Koenig of Vienna (who had come especially for the occasion), Metropolitan Meliton, Dean Alan Webster of Norwich representing the Archbishop of Canterbury, Mr Cornelius von Heyl, the

President of the Synod of the Protestant Church of West Germany, and the authors of the letter, of course – the international team. 'In Asia, we have been confirmed in our certainty that the wounds now tearing humanity apart can be healed,' begins the letter. 'Now we are leaving, after having discovered, in the very heart of deep distress, a people's astonishing vitality, and having encountered witnesses to another future for all. As a contribution to this future, the People of God has one possibility all its own: spread across the entire world, it can build up a parable of sharing in the human family. Such a parable will have force enough to propagate itself, shaking even the most immovable structures and creating communion throughout the whole human family. To lead the People of God into this radicalism of the Gospel you, now reading this letter, whether you be young or old, begin at once to make your own life a parable of sharing, by accomplishing concrete acts whatever the cost. Along this way, in Asia, many poor people, especially, are ahead of you.'

The letter has five parts, considering in turn the relationship of the People of God to its personal possessions, its living and working situation, the redistribution of the goods of the earth, and prayer. In the first part, the letter quotes Saint Ambrose of Milan, who as early as the fourth century preached that the earth belongs to all and not only to the rich. The People of God is asked to resist the urge to consume, and not to accumulate reserves for itself or its children. 'That is the beginning of injustice,' says the letter. More particularly, Church leaders, Christian communities, and families are called upon to establish a plan covering seven years, to deal radically with the problem of simplification. In the context of the Council of Youth, young people will go two by two to visit Church leaders and other Christians to talk about these seven-year plans. In the second part, the letter calls upon all the members of the People of God to turn their homes into places of constant welcome and to become aware of lonely people in their neighbourhoods. 'Invite people to share a meal,' reads the letter. 'A spirit of festival has more to do with simplicity than with large quantities of food.'

In the part about the working situation, the letter says that 'when career or competition, the desire for a high salary or consumer-demands are your basic reasons for working, you are not far from exploiting other people or being exploited yourself'. A little further on the authors emphasize the distribution of goods on the earth. 'A redistribution of wealth requires the industrialized nations to do more than just give away their surplus. The structures underlying international injustice must be changed at all costs.' To do this people are called to work on several different levels at once, says the letter. In this it is important to respect the methods of others. Some will struggle using political means; others will commit themselves in direct actions of solidarity with the victims of society. Finally, the letter states that the struggle for a better world cannot be sustained without communion with God. Prayer is a source of life. But 'words have gradually invaded churches, to such an extent that the worship of the People of God risks being an intellectual exercise rather than radiant communion'. That is why 'in silence let a living word of Christ be born in you, then put it into practice right away'. If the Church becomes a parable of sharing, so the letter concluded, then she will be, in the midst of the divided human family, a seed from which will spring a very different future for every human being. 'She will bring a hope which has no end.'

Throughout the week following the reading at Notre Dame, the Second Letter to the People of God was given ample coverage in the media all over the world. Groups everywhere trying to develop a new life-style in response to an overcrowded and overpolluted world saw it as a confirmation of their search. In Zurich and Madrid, where Brother Roger spoke in February and March 1977 in churches packed to the rafters, it was the most important topic during the preparatory group discussions. The periodical *Letter from Taizé*, which became a monthly beginning in January 1977, repeatedly gave it much space. The meeting in Zurich was especially striking on account of the great diversity of young people participating. Amidst bells, organ music, magnificently sung refrains, prayers, and readings, the young people heard the prior of Taizé say that homes of the dying exist not only in Calcutta, but also in the West with its countless victims of apathy, living dead all around us; that, as a Hindu leper told him in Calcutta, suffering is not a punishment but a visitation from God; that segregation is no longer acceptable, even (and above all) in the Church; that no one can say 'Justice, Justice' without practising it; that we are called to be witnesses to another future. Before the meeting in the Espiritu Santo church of Madrid, preparatory meetings had been held in San Sebastian (Basque Provinces), Huelva (Andalusia), and Besos (Barcelona). As a consequence, on the day of the meeting the Spanish capital saw young people arrive from literally all parts of Spain. Twelve neighbourhoods of Madrid were given the responsibility for welcoming them and providing them with board and lodging. Small groups were formed everywhere. People spoke of their lives and their commitments, the problems of the neighbourhood they were in, and how to make the parable of sharing a reality.

During the church service, in the presence of Cardinal Tarancon, Archbishop of Madrid, Brother Roger read a letter he had written in Asia for the young people of Spain. A continuation of 'Living Beyond Every Hope', it was entitled 'Witness to a Different Future', and in it Brother Roger discussed the Christian's attitude towards the past. 'No looking back,' exclaimed the prior during the service. 'That is a part of the Christian's freedom. He is only interested in what lies before him, what matters for him is hastening ahead of events.' In his talk he added: 'The Church can only be communion, and nothing else. She cannot model herself after governmental institutions, or become identified with a particular political party. If she lives out to the full her vocation to universality, to catholicity, she becomes a place where human liberty blossoms, an irreplaceable centre of sharing.'

Although in Taizé Easter 1977 was still characterized by the Second Letter to the People of God and its concrete applications, further stages of the Council of Youth were indicated. In the presence of 20,000 young people, Brother Roger announced that, together with a group of young Asians, he would spend time among the poorest inhabitants of Hong Kong, and then cross the border into China alone 'to pray for reconciliation and understanding among all human beings of goodwill'. It would be an expression of the desire of the young 'to lower the barriers which keep on re-forming between groups and peoples, isolating them from each other, rendering communion impossible'. The prior fixed his departure for the beginning of November 1977 following a meeting in the cathedral of Vienna. After a stop-over in the Philippines he would go to Holland, where a meeting in Breda would be organized for early December. At the end of April 1978 Brother Roger and some of the brothers were to spend two weeks of prayer in the town of Bari in the south of Italy, where they would live in a poor district of fishermen and masons, sharing the work of the neighbourhood, holding daily prayers, and offering hospitality to visitors. The prior also revealed that at the end of December 1978, the first international meeting of the Council of Youth for Europe outside of Taizé would take place, probably in Africa. And a few years later, a 'worldwide ecumenical gathering of youth' would be held in Taizé, where all those who had visited Taizé since the announcement of the Council in 1970 could be together for a few days.

On Holy Saturday evening it was mentioned as well that dif-ferent Churches and Christian communities had indicated that they too were anxious to reflect on the Second Letter to the People of God. For this reason, in the course of 1977, a number of bishops and other Church leaders visited Taizé. And it was stated that a 'conciliar stream' was assuring a continuity of prayer in many places, even among those harassed by the rhythms of a big city. This continuity of prayer was often rooted in apparently hopeless situations. Young people travelling around were discovering among the poorest of the poor how they could give a central place to sharing in their own lives. 'A serious analysis of our society and a struggle against the causes of injustice must go hand in hand with a

69

life among society's victims,' they stated. 'The poor are not only those without material things, but all who are rejected and outcast: the unemployed, political prisoners, handicapped people, the elderly, immigrant workers. . . .' They asked all who wished to do so to write a letter to Taizé during the coming months telling how they had already begun, or how they planned to begin, to put this sharing into practice.

Good Friday and Holy Saturday nights saw remarkable scenes in the Church of Reconciliation as the large icon of the Cross was laid on the floor before the altar, an image of Christ in the tomb. During the singing of *Adoramus te, Domine* ('We adore you, O Lord'), thousands of young people took turns kneeling around the Cross and kissing it. 'If Christ were not risen, would we be together here on this hill?' Brother Roger reflected in his Easter meditation. But young people had come together to celebrate the Council not only on that hill in Burgundy. On Mindanao, one of the largest islands of the Philippines, a number of people met at the same time for three days of prayer, discussion, and reflection on the theme 'Suffering and Hope'. In small groups they spoke of their experiences of struggle and suffering, and their visions of hope. They listened to workers at grips with situations of injustice, who lose their job if they speak out. They listened to those who work for the liberation of political prisoners, and to visitors from other countries. They listened too to young people expressing the same theme through drama and dance: the suffering of the present-day followers of Christ related to the suffering of the early martyrs. Every day, there were three times of common prayer. Simultaneously, an Easter celebration brought together on the island of Java Indonesians and visitors from abroad. Here too, time was spent in prayer, silence, sharing in small groups, singing and walking together. After the celebration in the Philippines, one of the young people who had taken part declared: 'The celebration gave birth in me to a new hope, not merely as speculation or an abstract idea, but a hope that is alive, and that possesses a dynamism which can shatter every structure of oppression. This hope has been planted;

it must now be watered by our prayers and our struggles to live.'

At Pentecost, the World Council of Churches celebrated in Lausanne, Switzerland, the fiftieth anniversary of Faith and Order. It was with the founding of this commission, in fact, that the ecumenical movement had begun. The jubilee was celebrated with festal Church services and addresses, at which both Roman Catholics and Protestants took part. The World Council asked Brother Roger and a group of those active in the Council of Youth to take charge of one of the services, on the eve of Pentecost. All the young people who were already planning to spend Pentecost at Taizé were asked to stop in Lausanne on their way. So that Saturday, many hours before the service began, an estimated 1500 French, German, English, Italian, and Swedish-speaking young people were already crowded in the square with its panoramic view in front of the ancient cathedral, while inside one of the brothers, physician cum musician of the community, was leading the hastily formed choir in a rehearsal of Cantate Domino, alleluia, alleluia, jubilate Deo ('Sing to the Lord . . . rejoice in God'). It sounded as if the new Jerusalem had finally descended; as if the imposing polyphonic choir, the orchestra, the organ, and the resounding trumpets were welcoming the King of Kings himself, there on that hill beside the Lake of Geneva; as if at last the Spirit had made himself master of them for ever.

After the service the young people kept watch until late at night in front of a simple, candle-lit icon in Lausanne Cathedral, while other young people – an estimated five hundred – undertook, in cars and buses, a 'pilgrimage' through the night to Taizé. That meant stopping and praying every hour and meeting all together twice in churches on the way. They finally arrived at Taizé at six o'clock in the morning.

What moved these young people in sneakers and blue jeans, with crosses on their breasts and flowers in their hands, to such spirituality? Brother Roger had tried to explain that the previous evening to the mass of people packed into the cathedral – sitting, kneeling, sitting on their heels, lying down, and even hanging in every nook and cranny. 'When they love the Church, these young people expect her to be aflame, they want her to kindle within us a fire to penetrate every dimension of our being, flesh-and-blood as well as spiritual,' Brother Roger had said. 'They are waiting for the Churches to set fire blazing across the whole earth, and, everywhere in the world, to make their own the concerns of every human being, to the very least of all. In doing this, are not Christians already witnesses to a different future?'

At the end of the service Brother Roger glanced at the nearby university building before, surrounded by a crowd of young and old, he got into the car which was to bring him back to Taizé that same evening. His thoughts remained his own, but they could be guessed at by anyone familiar with the history of Taizé. For it was in that building that, forty years ago, Roger chose a future which was to affect not only himself and his brothers, but the entire Church as well.

In mid-August 1977 Taizé was again in the news. Six Catholic bishops and young people from fifty different countries were in Taizé for a meeting which they unanimously set under the blood-red sign of El Salvador, where priests and lay people were being imprisoned, tortured, and killed. During a night and day of prayer in solidarity with the beleaguered people of that Latin American land, the bishops celebrated Masses and Brother Roger wrote an open letter to the President of El Salvador in which he called attention to the atrocious persecutions. 'A great many human beings everywhere in the world, particularly young Christians, are deeply disturbed by these happenings. In the name of human dignity, I appeal to the Christian religion you profess to urge you to use all the means at your disposal to cause such events to cease within the borders of your country.' The prior then revealed that he would ask two members of the intercontinental team to visit the president: 'If you refuse to receive them and my letter is left unanswered, I will do all in my power to go to El

Salvador myself.' News media all over the world published the letter, but the young people did not gain entry. The president replied in a telegram of several hundred words, in which he expressed his own point of view.

A month later Brother Roger addressed the National Eucharistic Congress of Italy, held that year in Pescara. On this occasion he caused eyebrows to rise once again by asking publicly for a transfiguration of the Vatican. 'The Bishop of Rome,' said the prior, 'is, it is true, weighed down with centuries of history. But if we flee his ministry, how will we enable him to undergo a transfiguration and exercise an ecumenical pastoral calling? Four and a half centuries ago, a part of Christendom did flee the bishop of Rome. Today, many non-Catholic Christians are coming to realize how necessary it is not to flee but to stand with him and those around him, so that all who reside in the Vatican undergo a transfiguration and become together a community that is a witness to others, an image to be reflected everywhere else. . . . Such a "witness-community" will spark a parable of communion, and will inevitably lead in its wake bishops and Church leaders, Catholics and non-Catholics, all over the earth.'

The weekend of 5 November saw the great Council of Youth celebration, which was held in Vienna after months of intensive preparation. Saturday afternoon, all the participants were welcomed at the parish hall of St Florian, a parish where the role of pastor had been replaced by a team of five, including two priests. Located in the centre of town, on a busy traffic artery, the parish is very much alive. There the hosts were waiting for the participants, who streamed in not only from all over Austria, but also from Germany, Yugoslavia, Poland, Switzerland, Italy, Spain, the Netherlands, and even Hong Kong. A thousand or so were expected, but twice that many arrived. But they all found places to stay, and some families who had offered hospitality were even left with no one to welcome! The next morning the participants, divided into groups, visited the so-called 'places of hope', which included prisons and refugee camps, families of immigrant workers, Amnesty International teams, traditional parish groups and other groups searching for a new life-style.

When the large prayer celebration began that evening the gigantic St Stephen's Cathedral had already been full to capacity for two hours. The building contained more people than it could reasonably hold, more than in any postwar service, according to the recollections of the older people who were there. An Austrian girl heard a woman say, 'Isn't it incredible: a football stadium is nothing compared to this!' The girl continued: 'Brother Roger was in the midst of all the praying people, surrounded by children who unselfconsciously snuggled up to him. . . . What he said betrayed a deep knowledge of the essential; his tone was calm, sometimes almost meditative, but every word was borne by an iron-clad conviction. In this world full of suspicion we have to bring back peace, he said, we have to break through barriers and prejudices, share with others rather than accumulate possessions, follow Christ without judging those who do not do so.'

After the weekend Brother Roger, together with a group of brothers and members of the intercontinental team, left for Hong Kong to write the 'Letter to All Generations' there. On the eve of the journey he explained why. 'If we are leaving again for Asia, it is in order to go further in the discovery of the meaning of sharing. Going to the border of China means placing oneself on one of the immense frontiers which keep humanity divided. We shall try to hear a word which God will speak to us there, through the poor people among whom we shall live and through all the people we meet.'

The stay had already been prepared by a brother who had arrived in Hong Kong a few months earlier. His task was to find a place for the group to stay and people who could help with the reflection on the letter. Just as the year before in Calcutta, various Churches offered buildings, but they were seldom located in the poorer districts. After weeks of searching, and when the first members of the group had already arrived, the Little Sisters of Jesus (of Charles de Foucauld) discovered a family which was about to

move from an old, makeshift shack on the waterfront to one of Hong Kong's many high-rise buildings, and which agreed to leave ahead of time. Immediately after evacuation the city normally tears down such a shack, but the brothers and young people were able to convince them that they should postpone the demolition for a few weeks. The entire group stayed in the shack, except for the girls, who slept on a neighbouring junk which was so leaky that it threatened to sink at any moment. Built on piles, the shack comprised two bare rooms and had no running water, electricity, or sanitary facilities. A hole in the floor served as a toilet, and to wash it was necessary to walk ten minutes to the nearest public showers. The group ate, slept, worked, and prayed on the wooden floor. During the day they welcomed young Chinese in ever-growing numbers, among whom were many workers; at night the rats crawled between and over them. The daily celebration of the Eucharist attracted much interest: on the next-to-last evening more than sixty young and old Chinese crowded into and around the dilapidated hut to assist at the Mass celebrated by the South Korean Cardinal Kim. During one of their last nights in Hong Kong the brothers and the young people narrowly escaped a fire that destroyed some fifty junks. With their cries they woke the sleeping junk-dwellers. As cries of anguish could be heard through the night dismay came over everyone. Brother Roger remembered: 'A question then sprang up in our hearts: does God wish people to suffer? No, God does not wish anyone to suffer or to die. God is no tormentor of the human conscience; he never punishes. No, through Christ, God suffers for and with every human being.' The day after the fire Brother Roger visited the junks that had been spared. The group had already become acquainted with the majority of the residents during the previous weeks. 'The profound goodness of all those Chinese people who offered us such a warm welcome will remain in me for ever,' said Brother Roger later. 'That is one of the characteristics of the Chinese people: they know how to love, they know how to suffer. Despite the apparent silence of God, those non-believers are inhabited by a Presence.'

76

After Hong Kong Brother Roger and some of the others visited a refugee camp in Thailand. There a portion of the country's 100,000 South Asian refugees live in a former prison, under constant surveillance by the Thai army, with no permission to leave or to receive visitors. The camp made such an indelible impression on the group that they decided to act. Various countries, such as the USA, France, Australia, Canada, Germany, Austria, and the Netherlands, do admit refugees from the camp with a certain regularity, but a great many other refugees are not eligible for such programmes. One such a case was a mother with twelve children whose husband had been killed in the war. The group decided to welcome a number of them to Taizé, and to make it possible for other such unfortunates, there and elsewhere in the world, to find a home. The action would be a continuation of 'Operation Hope', which in the 1960s enabled South American bishops to help poor peasants to begin farming co-operatives.

When Brother Roger returned to Europe with his brothers and the young people on Saturday, 10 December 1977, arriving in Breda in southern Holland, a Council of Youth celebration was already in progress and was turning the old city inside out. More than two thousand people had registered ahead of time for the weekend, half of them from Germany and Belgium. Others came from other parts of Holland, as well as France, Great Britain, America, Asia, and even New Zealand. More than a thousand families offered lodging, and some two hundred groups, communities, and organizations volunteered to exchange thoughts with the visitors on such topics as life-priorities, the testing of one another's ideals, and the letter that would be read publicly that same evening during a prayer service. The organizations and communities – called 'places of hope', as in Vienna – were very different from each other. 'Wherever people are struggling against injustice, wherever people share and pray together, there we see places of hope,' explained one of the organizers.

Before those who arrived went to find their host families, they registered in the municipal centre for foreign workers, which had been set up as a place of welcome. From behind long tables with card-trays young people from Taizé, Holland, and Flanders supplied information in different languages and provided the visitors with soup, coffee, and sandwiches. Buses arriving with foreigners led to hearty greetings and outpourings of emotion among people who had met earlier in Taizé. The crowd resembled one immense family which had come together for a reunion: small groups formed everywhere to share the latest news, brothers and young people lounged around or hurried by to take all kinds of last-minute measures, *bonjours* and hellos filled the air. Hidden away in a dark corner, an old woman was sitting and silently observing the noisy happening. Upon enquiry she seemed to have travelled for hours to be present for the celebration. She was 78, but felt young enough to want to participate in the whole thing at first hand. . . .

After the Roman Catholic Bishop of Breda had offered the brothers and young people a warm welcome in the afternoon, and after Brother Roger had answered the necessary questions at a press conference, at seven in the evening the common prayer service took place in Breda's largest hall: the regional vegetable market. The gigantic room was poorly equipped for such an event; that day, however, no pains were spared to give it a festive character. A wall of pineapple crates had been built on all sides, atop which innumerable candles flickered. Other fruit boxes were used to form rows of seats for the several thousand people who would fill the makeshift church.

Ubi caritas et amor, Deus ibi est. 'Where charity and love prevail, God is there.' From the mouths of the many-voiced mixed choir, accompanied by an impressive orchestra, the words sounded like a credo bridging the ages, a confession of love transcending dogmas and melting doubts. Many sang along, sitting, kneeling, or standing. Where just yesterday vegetable sellers were marketing their wares, today the Spirit was blowing, flowing, filling hearts, invisible and yet irresistible. *Veni Sancte Spiritus* rang out, and *Ostende nobis, Domine, misericordiam tuam*, 'Show us, Lord, your mercy'.

78

Us, but not just us here. Us too in the tormented land of Chile, in persecuted El Salvador, in the oppressed Philippines, in starving India. In all the places where people are suffering, where cries of despair are stifled. *Ostende nobis, Domine, misericordiam tuam!*

When the songs had ebbed away, the intercessions drawn to an end, and an episcopal word of welcome been spoken, Brother Roger took the microphone and addressed the crowd. 'Why did we go to share the living conditions of the poorest of the poor on the China Sea?' he asked. 'To make the most trying conditions which human beings have to undergo a part of our lives. It is dangerous to call for solidarity with the poor, to cry "justice, justice" while doing nothing. All who speak without acting destroy something essential in themselves. They run the risk of easing their own consciences while imprisoning those of other people.' Brother Roger then recounted what the group in Hong Kong had seen and experienced, and repeated the question: why the China Sea? 'For me, it was not a question of personal taste; I was not drawn by a natural inclination to leave Taizé and live under such conditions. My age, moreover, does not help matters any. But I am convinced of one thing: a Christian cannot live for himself; a Christian is asked not to save his own life, but to lose it for Christ and the Gospel.'

The 'Letter to All Generations', which grew out of the stay on the China Sea, was then read out. The letter had two new dimensions compared with previous texts. The first was that it laid an exceptionally strong accent on 'sharing'. An indication of that was this quotation from Saint John Chrysostom: 'The words "mine" and "yours" are empty of meaning; they do not express any reality. You are stewards of the goods of the poor, even when you have acquired them through honest labour or by inheritance.' Whereas in the previous letters – addressed to the People of God – the values, contemplation, struggle, and communion were visible in more or less equal measure, in this letter the communion among Christians was emphasized as a Gospel necessity in order to reach a universal human family. 'Once again in Asia,' said the letter, 'we

79

have been made aware how necessary it is that the Church, devoid of powerful means and without the support of human efficiency, be a source and become a ferment of friendship for all humanity.' To give this concrete form, the letter spoke of creating 'places of sharing', 'places offering simple hospitality, dwellings using the simplest of means'. These places of sharing will be composed of 'a few people or a community, a family or a couple', who are immersed in the contradictions of a society which engenders 'inequalities, the pursuit of profit, unbridled consumption, racial segregation, terrorism....' It will be necessary to 'live dangerously', since 'For Christ it is all or nothing. . . . Anyone who wants to save his life will lose it' (Mark 8, 34–8).

The letter was also characterized by the fact that it was addressed to both young and old. This was not only clear from the title, but also from the content: the letter urged that barriers between generations be torn down. 'In Asia, just as on the other continents, we have seen the consequences of this barrier: a rupture within the human personality, a lack of trust in others and in oneself, and, finally, the inability to realize a universal communion.'

But, one might ask, has not Taizé itself helped to maintain this rift, by addressing itself for years to 'young people', by convoking a 'Council of Youth', and so on? Moiz Rasiwala, one of the driving forces behind the Council of Youth, does not think so. He points out that it was said from the very beginning that this attention to the young in no way implied an exclusion of others. Now it has become even clearer, says Moiz, that this had to be emphasized once again.

Long after the meeting, lasting more than two hours, in the market-hall of Breda had ended, the strains of *Jubilate Deo* could still be heard. Within, the electric lights had already been dimmed, but the glow of the candles continued to form a halo around the figures of hundreds of men and women. Together with about thirty brothers of Taizé they knelt on the cold floor, some with their foreheads touching the ground, silent, praying for the Church, the world, and its uncertain future. The deep force of this universal posture drew unexpected tears from some older people present. A few yards away from those praying a boy, probably a student, was visibly going through the events in his mind. He peered over the heads of the stragglers like someone just beginning to have a vision.

Where there is love, there is God. Where love prevails, the smallest mustard seed flourishes. Beyond all lines of separation – between nations, races, and generations. Like a springtime bursting out, warming everything.

Taizé Today

Conversations with Brothers and Young Visitors

'I don't know how important prayer is to people when they arrive at Taizé, but the longer they stay the more important it becomes for them. Maybe it's because of the fixed times of prayer, around which the whole day is built. Three times each day everything comes to a halt. Just like in some Muslim countries where I've been.'

The speaker is thirty-nine-year-old Moiz from India. Moiz first heard about Taizé during the sixties, when he was studying astrophysics at the Sorbonne in Paris. He returned several times to the hill in Burgundy 'to meet people who were conscious of their social responsibilities'. He made some good friends among the brothers, with whom he maintained an extensive correspondence after his return to India in 1970. There, in the region of Bombay, he joined a group working for the development of the country. He never talked about Taizé, but there too, according to Moiz, Taizé was a great support for him. 'People in Taizé encouraged me and called me a sign of hope. That meant a lot, because it really was a story of death and resurrection.' In 1974, shortly before the opening of the Council of Youth, Moiz received a letter from Brother Roger inviting him to come to Taizé with his wife and small child, and to commit himself directly for a time to the Council. Moiz accepted, and between 1974 and 1977 he developed into one of the moving forces behind the Council of Youth. He served the young visitors as an inspiring organizer and discussion-leader, and at the same time he gave invaluable support to the prior and the

TAIZÉ

other brothers involved with the Council of Youth. Together with Brother Roger he took part in several European Council celebrations, and in 1976 he collaborated with the group in Calcutta when they wrote the Second Letter to the People of God.

Moiz was discussing the spiritual life at Taizé with Mildrède, a twenty-seven-year-old French woman. It was a fascinating experience, not only because of the totally different cultures from which they come, but also because they represent two such different types: Moiz is small, slightly built, and relatively inconspicuous; Mildrède is tall, pretty, and striking. Moreover, Mildrède did not consciously seek out Taizé like Moiz, but came upon it by chance, through a friend in 1970, at the time that the Council of Youth was first announced. Before coming she expected nothing in particular from the visit, but as soon as she saw the Church of Reconciliation, with its Roman Catholic and Orthodox chapels, she was enchanted. 'All at once in that church I saw the power and the beauty of Christian unity. What struck me after that was the common prayer, and the quality of the discussions here. Taizé seemed to be a place where people dared to take off their masks, where they dared to talk about prayer, silence, and themselves.'

After she had returned to her home in Le Mans, Mildrède decided to finish her English language studies in the United States. 'Taizé had opened my eyes and widened my horizon. I wanted to meet young Americans on a deeper level than people usually do. I wanted to tell them about the spiritual search of young Europeans, the Council of Youth, and the universe that had opened up for me here.' Her plans worked out, and she became a teaching assistant in an American college. On her return to France she started working as a teacher, but Taizé attracted her so much that a year later she decided to make herself available for a few years to help directly with the Council of Youth. With other young adults she lived for two years in a black ghetto in Philadelphia, travelled in Alaska, and spent the better part of a year in Africa, where she formed part of the temporary fraternity in Nairobi during the

84

fifth Assembly of the World Council of Churches. 'To make contact with other groups of young people, to spread the "joyful news", and to live a Christian presence among the poor,' she explained. Returning to Taizé in 1976, she served for a while as a leader in several discussion groups.

'When I listen to all these young people here and elsewhere, I find that many experience prayer, especially the common prayer here, as a real discovery. The praying and singing in different languages especially helps them to see the universality of Christ's message. But also the dimension of silence. I've spoken with Jewish people and other non-Christians who were deeply impressed by the periods of silence here and who have commented that is the only time when all the barriers to communication fall down. When we're all the same, whether we speak French or not.' Why? 'Because silence teaches us to be ourselves. Unfortunately most people never make time for it. I didn't either, in the past. I didn't even know that silence existed. Since I came to Taizé, however, silence has become an essential part of my daily life. Even when I'm at home or somewhere else. And I know that I'm growing in that dimension. For me silence is no longer just empty time or listening to the distracting voices within. It's much more placing myself in the presence of God.'

Does this mean that in Taizé prayer takes priority over everything else – discussions, social involvement, community life? That Taizé wants above all else to be an oasis of spirituality? For Moiz the answer is obvious. 'Absolutely,' he assured me. 'Prayer takes absolute priority. And that brings with it a characteristic atmosphere. Is it artificial, a kind of gimmick? I don't think so; for the community, prayer is the centre of their existence.' And for the visitors? 'Gradually you see them becoming aware that here prayer is something that really matters, not just something superficial, but part of their very being. After a few days many visitors come and tell you that they have learned to pray here, that they've discovered the meaning of prayer, or at the very least that they like to attend the services, because they find them a remarkable experience.

Which of course doesn't mean that everybody goes to absolutely every service.'

It is a remarkable phenomenon, this interest in prayer, even more so because, in the countries from which most visitors to Taizé come, many of the Churches loudly bewail the decline in church-going by younger members of parishes and congregations. How pessimistic people in general are about this state of affairs was made clear to me recently by a Roman Catholic professor, secretary of a national Church council, a man better informed than most about the religious situation in his country. 'If the tendency of the last years continues,' he said, 'then twenty-five years from now the institutional Church will be finished. There will be no more ministers and, above all, no more church-goers. With the exception of some very conservative groups, the official Church seems to be on its last legs.'

What attracts young people from all over the world to Taizé, one asks, when they pay no attention to their own Church at home? *Moiz*: 'Here in Taizé we have no explanation of why young people don't go to church at home. Like everybody else, we are aware of the fact. Just as we notice that they pray here on a massive scale, sometimes ten thousand at a time. Why? I have the feeling that it has something to do with meaningfulness. The young hesitate more than their elders to do something if its meaning is not immediately evident to them. When they can't find the meaning of a worship service or a prayer, they react right away and pull out. Prayer has to have a central meaning in their life, they must be able to come to grips with it existentially. Their acceptance or rejection of prayer is related to the general tendency towards subjectivism, which is a sign of our times. The interest shown in prayer here is also connected with the presence of brothers for whom the common prayer means a great deal. That stimulates the others. Whenever people lead an authentic life together, a kind of invisible bond is created, a communion, that makes itself felt and becomes a point of attraction for others. That phenomenon is not only found in Taizé, but in many large and small religious communities, even in

86

local Church groups. Taizé is just a place where it's more visible, more tangible.' Do the young themselves ever explain why they go to church at Taizé and not at home? *Moiz*: 'I've never found one single explanation, but rather a whole complex of personal motives. The reason most often heard is, I think, the silence, which forms an integral part of the liturgy. But also the freedom to attend the services or not, to adopt the posture you feel like in praying: kneeling, sitting, bowing down. Prayer then becomes not only an intellectual exercise but something you do with your whole body. Many say they find that the liturgy, the singing especially, attracts them. And also the cycle of the liturgical year which is followed here.' *Mildrède*: 'Prayer in Taizé is an important part of the rhythm of a day. In this way a close bond is created between contemplation and activity, between what you think and what you do. I've noticed in conversations, by the way, that lots of young people go to church, at home and elsewhere, at times when no services are being held. What they reject is more the routine and the conventional style of the celebrations than prayer itself. They just have no time for performances which mean nothing to them.' Are there no such performances in Taizé? *Mildrède*: 'The content and the form of prayer are frequent topics of discussion here, which proves that prayer is really alive for young people, otherwise they wouldn't talk about it. But then over and over again the word freedom comes up, the freedom to be oneself which the brothers allow others and themselves. One of my friends from India was afraid when he came here that the brothers would influence him to become a Christian. To his surprise they did just the opposite: they tried to learn from him.'

It also seems an obvious paradox that, at a time when almost everywhere in the world the Roman Catholic Church is simplifying its liturgy – some would even say 'protestantizing' it – the originally Protestant Community of Taizé has a liturgy that now and then reminds one of the Catholic liturgy before the Council. And yet Taizé attracts people in spite of this liturgy – or is it because of it?

Mildrède: 'Yes, because of it. Because you realize that you can be joyful not only out of church, but in it as well. Common prayer exists to celebrate the joy of being a Christian, and yet many Churches seem to have forgotten this. So often in such Churches you find worship in which the pastor or a team of people have come up with every possible gimmick for attracting people, and yet you feel that it all means nothing to the organizers themselves. In Taizé the community has a burning desire for Christian unity, and that comes across in their prayer, which, by the way, is no ego-trip or shutting out of the world: it goes out to those suffering in the world. To answer your question, I find the pattern of the prayer here very simple, certainly, but traditional as well.'

Moiz: 'Many visitors find church services at home cold and unattractive. That's because the Church has for a long time underemphasized the emotional side of prayer. But I think that now some people are rediscovering this important dimension. They react against church services that appeal exclusively to their intellect, not to their heart, where there is no room for contemplation, for all that lies beyond the reach of reason. Those young people want worship in which we transcend the limits of our intellect, which brings us into contact with mystery, contemplation. I think there is also an Eastern element in all this, by the way.'

Could that be the reason why the worship at Taizé attracts so many people? Eastern mysticism is very 'in' among Western youth. Books on the subject sell like hot cakes. *Moiz*: 'Perhaps. But the brothers did not develop their prayer with this in view. They haven't changed the basic form of their liturgy since the community began.' Does Moiz find a marked leaning towards Eastern mysticism in Taizé, and what does he think of it? 'There is clearly a great need for something in that direction, but as an Indian I am somewhat disturbed as well. The need comes from a two-fold tendency in European society: on the one hand the search for an emotional outlet in face of the growing rationalism of industrialized society, and on the other the subjectivism, the desire to experience everything directly. What scares me most of all is that in the West Eastern mysticism is not integrated within the existing culture, as it is in my country. People take a slice of the cake – the direct religious experience – and leave all the rest. This creates a sort of alienation. You can't separate the experience from the rest just like that. You can't do without the backbone of mental substructures that accompanies the mysticism over there. I would much rather see European young people rediscover their own monastic tradition. First of all because it's very beautiful and secondly, because it belongs much more to European life and thought.'

Aren't a growing number of young people already doing just that? Aren't the guest-houses of contemplative orders like the Benedictines and Trappists a clear illustration of this? Only doesn't it happen because the Church throughout the world – with excuses for the apparent contradiction – has brushed aside mysticism to such an extent? What is left in Protestantism of early Christian mysticism? And in modern Catholicism? Are we not well on our way to the one-dimensional thinking and feeling of the humanist?

Moiz: 'In a lot of churches, indeed, little *is* left of mysticism. On the other hand, you have to keep in mind that mysticism has always been practised more in the contemplative orders you mentioned than in the churches. Just as in India it's more likely to be found in the ashrams than in the temples. But that the need for mysticism is perhaps greater today than ever before is obvious to me.' To what extent does Taizé respond to this? 'Insofar as Taizé has left the mystery intact in the structure of its prayer. But I'd rather speak here about spirituality than about mysticism as such.'

Mildrède agreed for the most part with Moiz, but with a different emphasis. During their stay in the United States she often came into contact with 'mystical' groups. What struck her most was their hunger to have their deepest questions answered. 'The "hows" have all been answered. The how of the mechanical, industrial world, the how to make money. But not the fundamental "whys" of life. I think that's why today many young people won't go on until they have grasped the deeper values of life.' Mysticism as a reaction to the welfare state? 'I think that more and more young people are becoming aware that having more does not make you happier in the end. I have never met happier people than I did in poor neighbourhoods of Mexico and Africa. Not that I would want to be poor, but poor people sometimes know how to give a quality to their lives that I've never seen anywhere else. For me they were an anticipation of the kind of Church I'd like to see. Really living beyond every hope.'

But how do you live, concretely, a life beyond every hope? Do you do it with an impressive spirituality? Is that the appropriate method for fighting the fire in the forest of humanity? How does it help an oppressed, starving peasant in Colombia that in Taizé a thousand of his fellow-Christians are reflecting on the mystery of their existence? Isn't that a form of escapism? A flight from social reality?

Mildrède: 'The theme of the Council of Youth is struggle *and* contemplation. And that theme was born of a very strong intuition, on each of the continents. I am well aware that our generation, in the face of so much injustice in the world, is quickly inclined to say: For God's sake, do something! Then we go and join a social movement, a socio-economic study group, a political party or something. That's absolutely all right with me, as long as at the same time we don't underestimate those whose commitment for others takes the form of praying for them. Otherwise once again you create an either-or situation: *either* you are involved, *or* you pray. Then prayer becomes a form of escapism. What matters for us here in Taizé is linking struggle and contemplation, not considering them separately, even if in your particular situation you are inclined to emphasize the former more than the latter. The discovery that it's a back-and-forth movement, a reciprocity. That's where its strength lies. If you dedicate yourself only to activities, you are easily submerged by them, you become an activist and you lose the fundamental inspiration and energy which at that moment is exactly what you need. On the other hand, the same thing is true for those who lose themselves in contemplation and close their eyes to the suffering around them. The two dimensions keep each other in equilibrium.'

But doesn't the kind of prayer you pray have something to do with it? Shouldn't contemplation be something which opens towards struggle? As opposed to a kind of meditative dreaming which, out of a desire for self-satisfaction, strives for a 'religious experience'.

Moiz: 'Christian contemplation will continually find itself at the crossroads between the outside world and one's inner world, between the macrocosm and the microcosm within yourself. The Eastern attitude in contemplation is one of self-fulfilment, or self-realization. But for me that is not a Christian attitude. I don't believe that mystery can be present in prayer unless there is an element of communion, of solidarity with the suffering of the world around you. The world must find a place in the heart of your prayer. That is basic to being a Christian. The God of the Bible is first and foremost the Lord of history. In Eastern religions there is no experience of a God who loves the world so much that He commits himself to it.' So no ego-trip spirituality? 'Naturally someone may find it necessary at a certain period in his life to experience his own fullness and to go very deeply into himself. But to concentrate only on that. . . . Maybe in India. But India also shows how badly the social dimension fares in a culture that is concerned with the spiritual alone.'

What is meant then by contemplation in Taizé? And how does it keep the young people day after day in the Church of Reconciliation, the retreat-house, the zones of silence? What do you do with the silence, anyway? Is there a technique? Like yoga, for instance?

Moiz: 'No, no technique. I see it as a continuing dialogue with God.' But how can you have a dialogue with someone who doesn't answer? 'A monologue, if you like, but a violent one, as in the Old Testament. Such as: why do you do *that* and not *that*, and so on. The very personal confrontation with a personal God. The silence is there to make you empty. Mary was and she was filled with Christ. In that way she made herself available. We do that too: we

make ourselves available to God. And when you are filled with
Christ, you go to others and offer Him to them. Out of sheer joy.'
When I look around in Taizé, I can't avoid the impression that
many people don't know how they're supposed to handle the
silence. 'I'm sure that's so. But we emphasize that the young
people don't need to worry about it. When you abandon yourself
completely, so to speak, to make room in yourself for the Spirit of
God, when you have so much trust in the Spirit, well then, the
power of God will be stronger in you than the spirit of the world. In
spite of all your hesitations, doubts, mistakes, and so forth. Most
young people find silence one of the most important experiences
here.'

Mildrède: 'Contemplation taught me to accept my dependence
on God and to see it as a relationship of love. A relationship of
growing trust which makes you able to abandon yourself completely to God. Often I pray: I lay my hand in yours, God, into
your hand I commit my spirit. That dimension is just as important
for me as a father's hand is for his child. The child knows that that
hand will never lead him in the wrong direction. Little by little I've
been discovering that God leads us on to greater happiness. But
then we have to give up our own ideas and let God work in us. For
me silence is the focus for that.'

*

The heavens declare the glory of God
and the firmament praises the works of his hands.
Day proclaims it to day
and night recounts it to night;
with never a word nor a sound,
never a voice to be heard;
yet their song goes round the earth
and their words to the end of the world.

Day has just dawned as the nineteenth Psalm rises melodiously
from the still somewhat sleepy crowd. The bells of Taizé have

already declared the glory of God as they rang out over the houses, barns, and tents of the hill in Burgundy. Their message was heard everywhere and long trails of silent church-goers formed, walking with the slackened pace of human ants on their way to the same meeting-place. There they sat on their heels, heads hidden in their hands, or threw themselves flat on the ground, as their brother Jesus had done in the Garden of Gethsemane. Even if their voices can hardly be heard and their words do not reach to the end of the world, their very presence states what their semi-conscious minds can hardly express: that they know themselves to be dependent while others fancy themselves almighty; that they want to be awake while others are asleep; that they are conscious of belonging to a greater kingdom than this village, this country, this world; that day will proclaim it to day, the morning prayer to the midday prayer and that again to the evening vigil; and that in this way brothers and visitors see their worship taken up in the unbroken stream of the ages, the same stream which has carried to them the spiritual experience of past generations.

Taizé stands in this stream, just as the first Christian communities stood in it, when they came together daily for prayer in Jerusalem. It was new and yet it was not, for the roots of that Christian prayer in fact already lay in ancient Israel. In this way, too, throughout the history of Christianity spirituality has been a mixture of the old and the new, of tradition and contemporaneity. Again and again the heritage of the fathers has been taken up, and elements introduced – or emphasized – which appealed to believers at that juncture. Our liturgies are no exception to this.

Taizé stands in a very special way in this evolution, because it has not chosen the traditional elements of its liturgy simply from the heritage of one particular denomination in this century, but has made use of the whole, variegated treasury of almost twenty centuries as a source for the rediscovery of valuable words and melodies. The result is that almost every Christian recognizes himself in the liturgy of Taizé: the Reformed in the Psalms set to music, the Lutheran in certain of the chorales, the Eastern Orthodox in the Beatitudes and the polyphonic alleluia, the Roman Catholic in the text of the Eucharist, as well as in some Gregorian chants and the often-sung (in Latin!) *Veni Creator Spiritus*. On the other hand, the liturgy has been constructed in such a way that it nourishes and stimulates the day-to-day Christian task of love and service in the world. The brothers try to achieve this by a clear use of words, and this in a number of different living languages; by reviewing the liturgy regularly, by removing certain parts and adding new ones, and so keeping the whole alive; by mentioning the needs of the world directly in the prayer and so bringing them to people's attention; and by giving those present an active part in the service. This last is especially important. The practice in some monasteries, where the style of the monks' singing in choir makes it in fact impossible for visitors to take part, is unthinkable in Taizé. Naturally the musicians of the community try to reach the highest attainable artistic level. But never at the cost of the congregation's participation. In Taizé everyone joins in the singing and the prayers as far as possible, even if he or she does not know the French language, which is, after all, the principal language.

An obviously traditional aspect of the liturgy in Taizé are the times when the common prayer is held. The idea is that our life is marked by a rhythm of darkness and light, day and night, sleeping and waking. A rhythm that is not foreign to the Bible, either. On the one hand you find there the peaceful alternation of work and rest, on the other the constant challenge to stay awake and pray with Christ in Gethsemane. Again and again the People of God are confronted with the temptation to prefer darkness and death to the light of Christ. Christians have always watched and prayed at times when the alternative is most evident: at sunset, sunrise, and the astronomical middle of the day.

Usually those are also the times when people come together to pray in Taizé. To recall by and with the universal Church the burial, resurrection, and glorification of the Son of God. The rhythm becomes evident in the course of the week as well, particularly on Friday, the day Jesus died, on Saturday, the Sabbath during which he rested in the tomb, and on Sunday – or more precisely Saturday night – the moment of the resurrection. In the course of the year, the cycle is recognizable in Advent, Lent, and the Easter season. In addition, the Taizé liturgy accentuates the communion of saints – the Virgin Mary, Mother of Jesus, John the Baptist, the apostles and evangelists, and Stephen, the first martyr. Taizé motivates this devotion by explaining that in its saints the Church honours above all else their faithfulness, and their complete harmony of faith and life; they were visibly bearers of Christ for those around them, including their persecutors.

That in and through all this the Scriptures play an important role hardly needs to be demonstrated, especially since the original roots of the community are in the Protestant tradition. The liturgy of Taizé is Biblical through and through, as is evident from the structure of the daily worship services. Normally they begin with a number of verses from a Psalm, which is sung by everyone. A Scripture reading follows, in the morning from the Old Testament and the Gospels, in the evening from a letter of Paul or one of the other apostles. (In the summer this order is inverted.) The response to the reading is another text from the Bible, sung by one of the brothers and repeated in part by the congregation. After that the Church of Reconciliation becomes silent. That silence lasts a long time, at least ten minutes, sometimes more. Everyone who wants to can allow the Bible reading to penetrate deeper into himself, verifying with it his own daily life or that of the world around him. He can converse with God in the depths of his heart, or he can make himself empty and simply keep watch, without words, in self-abandonment.

The second half of the service, centred around intercessory prayer, usually begins with a litany. After each intercession the whole congregation responds, *Kyrie eleison*, 'Lord, have mercy!' Following an Eastern Orthodox custom they prolong the final chord as an accompaniment for the following intercession. After a short collect which changes once a week, specific intentions are mentioned. In the morning they concern a particular country, and in the evening they are taken from a list of names of suffering people and friends of the community. For example, if one day a visitor from Thailand is present, he may be asked to pray for people he knows; he will pray aloud in his own language. For the last few years the whole liturgy has become so international that most prayers are said or sung in a number of different languages, which vary from one service to the next. The languages most often used are French, English, German, Spanish, Italian, and Dutch. The service concludes with a hymn and a short prayer by the prior, in which he invokes God's blessing; at midday he usually improvises a somewhat longer prayer. Not until the last notes of the organ – or sometimes the gentler tones of a guitar – have died away do the brothers and their guests leave the church. The exception is morning prayer, which is followed by a distribution of the Eucharist for which all gather around the altar. On Sunday mornings the Eucharist is celebrated in a festive manner. The Saturday evening service is likewise more festive than the others, because then the groups of visitors, who during the past week have been practising instrumental and vocal music, offer the results of their work in worship. In addition, at the end of Saturday evening service a short ceremony takes place which many consider the high point of the week. First a candle is lit in anticipation of one's own resurrection, and the flame is passed from one person to another until the whole Church of Reconciliation is a sea of light. Then the Gospel of the Resurrection is read, after which everyone extinguishes his or her candle and leaves the church in silence. Until about 1970 it was the custom to hold a brief sermon during the Sunday morning service. Today this is less common. In its place, one evening a week, usually Thursday or Friday, Brother Roger remains in the church after prayer and speaks to the assembled guests. His words are simultaneously translated into English and German, and often into Italian, Spanish, Dutch, and other languages. On these occasions young people are invited to speak as well. Afterwards, anyone who wants to say goodbye personally to the prior waits to see him in a line which often comes to an end well after midnight. Standing near one of the early Christian icons in the church, he tries to say something essential to each visitor, listening to his or her problems or praying with him or her by the feeble light of a few wax candles.

Anyone reading this could form the impression that the Taizé liturgy is an inorganic jumble of arbitrary traditional and modern elements. A kind of least-common-denominator liturgy, product of a forced and unripe ecumenism. Such an impression would be unjust, for the integration of the different influences which Taizé has undergone over the years has gone so far that the great majority of visitors experience the liturgy of Taizé as extremely authentic. For anyone who studies the history of that liturgy, that too comes as no surprise. Since its foundation, the Taizé Community has evolved from a narrowly Protestant group to a monastic community in which now almost all the major Christian traditions – with the exception of the Eastern Orthodox – are represented. This drastic evolution, however, has taken place very gradually, and little by little it has had its repercussions in the liturgy. Every element has grown into it. Sometimes quite spontaneously. Once in Taizé there lived a Bulgarian monk with an exceptionally deep and rich voice, who often sang the Gospel during the worship services. One day he added a Bulgarian alleluia to it, which everyone found so beautiful that it has remained in use until today. It has become known as the 'Taizé alleluia'. Occasionally a brother from Taizé travelling somewhere in the world hears a beautiful melody in a monastery and writes it down. The melody is then eagerly tried out in the Church of Reconciliation.

Naturally one should not imply that the liturgy of Taizé is never the object of criticism. On the contrary, some of the resistance against it is considerable. For example, in Taizé I personally met a Swiss church group which had to leave prematurely because their leader was so shocked by the liturgy that he could not bear to remain any longer on the hill. The man, who was basically very friendly and full of goodwill, was a typical representative of that branch of Protestantism which believes that worship should

be limited to the proclamation of the Word of God as it is laid down in the Bible. He considered meditation and litanies a reprehensible form of Romish mysticism and as such practically the work of the devil. His wife, moreover, was highly offended by the young visitors' clothing and their unconventional postures during prayer. Even after long discussions she could not comprehend why this is allowed. Other critics reproach the brothers of Taizé for ignoring the secularization which during the last decades should have purified the Western Church from what they generally term 'idolatry'. They think that all kinds of sacred elements, which since the time of German theologian Dietrich Bonhoeffer have been excluded from the Church (like the making and honouring of all images of God except interhuman activity), are being brought in again by the back door. The brothers, however, resolutely deny any desacralization of prayer. They think that a thorough desacralization would lump Christians together with humanists and put an end to the transcendent dimension of faith. In his book *Violent for Peace* Brother Roger replies to the modernistic notion that God is only to be found in other human beings – in the horizontal dimension, in other words. 'Is not God then once again imprisoned in a particular language? What do these new formulations accomplish besides changing the terms? Formerly God was found only in the heights; today he is discovered only in the depths of the personality. . . .' Worship in Taizé is definitely not a kind of Sunday school for adults, as the German theologian Dr Andreas Stökl points out in his dissertation *Taizé* (Hamburg, 1975). 'Their chapel is neither the market place of Billy Graham with human beings viewed as mission-objects, nor the classroom of a didactic church filled with over-grown schoolchildren,' Stökl writes. For example, during prayer services the brothers refuse to read from newspapers or political commentaries, as is frequently done in grass-roots communities and avant-garde parishes. 'Our common prayer,' writes Brother Roger, 'is like a mosaic – some consider it beautiful, others shapeless. What one person finds meaningless speaks to someone else. One appreciates the Psalms, or the long silences following the Scripture readings, or the litanies. There are those who wait above all for the organ music at the end of the service. To each his own. To expect everything to be experienced with equal intensity, even by one person, is utopian.'

Yet what some people have long considered utopian has become reality in the hands and hearts of many young Taizé-goers. This is evident from an article by Rita and Georg from Germany, who talk about their life at home:

'Several weeks ago, we began a new experience. We go into our room in the evening, and we sit or kneel on the floor, with a cross or a candle in front of us. First we listen to some music, an organ piece that we like a lot. Then one of us reads a short passage from an epistle, and we remain in silence. At the end, we sing or we play something on the flute. Usually there is just the two of us, though sometimes we invite friends.

'We believe that what we mean by contemplation must not be limited to prayer times. These moments of silence are like bridge-heads for us; we are trying to fill our day-to-day lives with what we experience in the silence. Contemplation is a way towards a new dimension in our lives. It is like living in the same house for several years, and suddenly uncovering a door in the house and beyond the door new spaces that you had never known were there. It is in these new spaces that we are rediscovering ourselves. Within us we are discovering new sources of joy, unsuspected possibilities for commitment, resources of imagination for starting out afresh. We are rediscovering a simplicity which helps us to be really true. Further, we are discovering within us a poverty and a vulnerability. We can see that we are not what we seem to be, that we are not as important as our activities may make us appear, that our hands are empty and not full. At the same time, contemplation means a meeting with Christ, and the discovery of his traits in ourselves brings us closer to him.

'We find contemplation to be less a goal than a starting-point for giving our lives.'

That there are at present young people all over the world who in this or a similar way are trying to 'convert' themselves from within by the Spirit of God, using this as a starting-point to make the world around them a place fit to live in is, humanly speaking, due to the presence of and the light from the Community of Taizé. Visitors to Taizé may commit themselves totally for a week, a month, a year, or even longer, to God and his Church; the brothers have literally staked their whole lives on this. They have given up a large part of their personal freedom, renounced possessions (thereby also power and prestige), and sacrificed what may be the greatest happiness known to the human race: the warmth of an exclusive love.

How can a human being achieve this, the outside observer asks himself. What leads someone to make such a 'contract', to enter into such an existential bond? And why should they do this in Taizé and not one of the thousands of other churches or monasteries in the world? I put these and other questions to three brothers – who for this rare occasion agreed to an interview.

The youngest of the three is twenty-nine years old. Born and raised in an Asian village, his features are typically Oriental: coal-black hair, dark eyes, olive skin, relatively small and slender in build. He radiates a tranquillity which, whether you like it or not, immerses you in contemplation.

While he was still a boy, this young brother wanted to become a priest. After seven years of study in a diocesan seminary, he went to a poor and dilapidated village several hours away by train. There he took a teaching job, intending to acquire some pastoral experience. By pure chance he met in that village a Taizé brother, who had been working in Mother Teresa's Homes for the Dying and then with the fraternity at Chittagong, Bangladesh. 'Together we took a train to another village and during that hour, in that overcrowded compartment, the brother impressed me very much,' he said. 'I wanted to become a priest, but not a mediocre one. I didn't feel at ease, I was continually hesitating between a career as a clerical social worker and life in a world of pious dreams. I confided my problems to the brother, who suggested it might be a good idea to interrupt my studies for a few months and help with the preparations for the Council of Youth in Taizé.'

The seminarian took his advice and arrived at Taizé in August 1973. There he lived among the guests and became active as a leader of group discussions. 'In Asia I had spent several months in a refugee camp in Bangladesh, and that experience not only influenced me deeply, it was also very useful to me here,' he said. Eventually he decided to remain in Taizé, becoming a member of the community in 1974. What, more than anything else, led him to make that decision? His reply, when it came, was calm and measured. 'I wanted to give myself totally. And I believed – and still do believe – that a Christian cannot do so outside of a community. I discovered community life in Taizé, and an ecumenical community at that. In 1965, in the seminary, I had read the documents of the Second Vatican Council on ecumenism. In Taizé I read them once again, and I was struck by the passages I had underlined in the seminary. In the Community of Taizé those words had become reality. I knew then that the Spirit was leading me.'

What had Taizé shown or taught him since that time that he hadn't experienced in a village church in Asia? The question evidently embarrassed him; like his fellow brothers he avoids as much as possible any criticism of the official Churches. Carefully he replied: 'Taizé taught me that a life of faith is essentially a life that has to be put into practice. A life in which you let your faith transform everyday reality. That means both spiritual life and involvement in society. Taizé gives you room for both.' But why Taizé? 'Every time I talk with young people here, I have the feeling that all I have to offer them is my silence. By our silent lives here we try to be mirrors in which young people can recognize their own treasures, so that they become aware of what they have to contribute.' But Taizé offers more than just silence. 'Simplicity also, maybe. When we pray we all sit on the same floor: the brothers, the guests, everybody. In society first you are a doctor, a lawyer, or a student, and only afterwards a human being. Here you are a human being first, and only then everything else. Here love of God and love of men belong together; at home young people often consider it artificial that those loves are experienced separately, the one at church and the other at home, at work, and so on.'

At the end of 1976 the young brother returned to his country for a few weeks to be ordained a priest, in the presence of Brother Roger. Does he now see a growing closeness between the official Churches because of and within the ecumenical Community of Taizé? 'Within the community we seldom talk about the denominations we come from. There is so much more uniting than separating us.' The Roman Catholic hierarchy doesn't always seem to think so. . . . 'Ecumenism in the Church will have to grow from within. But it must be that way, so that you don't lose sight of the other. To be concerned about that is also a part of Christian love. The Church at ground-level may well tug at the top. But always with love. For the Church is top *and* ground-level. If the two become separated, then there is no more Church.'

Another brother who has something to say about that comes from Germany. He is one of the brothers who take care of the retreat-house in Taizé, the place where visitors can spend a week in solitude and silence. Such visitors include priests, ministers, and others working in the Church who from time to time need to reflect anew upon their work and their spiritual sources. They can have daily conversations with one of the brothers at the retreat-house.

The German brother comes from a milieu which he describes as 'de-Christianized'. His family was Lutheran, but they seldom went to church. 'There was absolutely no frame of reference for a monastic vocation,' he said. 'I never even thought about it as a boy. Christian community was unknown to me: the monastic orders I had heard about were either too pious for my tastes, or completely unconnected to the existing society. The only form of community I experienced was on the football field and in other team sports.'

The brother studied at a commercial school in Germany, after which he taught English, history, and geography at a school in Upper Volta. 'Living and working in the worst slums of West Africa, I experienced a living Church for the first time,' he said. 'I heard about Taizé while I was in Africa, and decided to go there for a few days upon my return to Europe.' He did that in 1966, while he was working as a social worker in a home for working-class boys south of Paris. 'Here I experienced the community for which I had been looking for years: community life *and* prayer.' In 1967 he became a brother, a little more than six months after the first large meeting for young people took place on the hill. Since then he has devoted himself to work with the young, the last few years especially with retreatants.

From this experience he has been able to draw some remarkable conclusions. 'The fact that young people go to church less often today doesn't mean in the least that they are any less interested in faith,' he assured me. 'Maybe they don't go to traditional Church services precisely because the existential question of faith weighs so heavily on them. By that I don't mean to say anything against those Churches; many of their members take their faith very seriously. But because of the confusing age we live in, such people are often not able to change much in the Church, while others sometimes want change in too radical, too aggressive a fashion.' What do young people find in Taizé, then, that attracts them so much ? 'A place where people listen to one another. Where you meet committed people. People do not expect us, the brothers, to know all about everything, to be experts in politics, sociology, theology, and so on. Just that we remain faithful to our vocation and live it as a visible sign for others. That we are here because of Christ, who is in fact the living source of our lives. Christ was the man for others, and at the same time he was the revelation of God's love. From that follow the two dimensions: struggle and contemplation. When you have a joyful vision of the Kingdom of God, it's easier for you

to look forward to it with joy.' But how is this possible in an age of nuclear weapons, torture, and pollution? 'A German once said, "After Auschwitz no more alleluias can be sung". But he forgot that right there in Auschwitz there were people singing alleluias. That it is possible to transcend the reality of the present moment without fleeing from it.'

A Dutch brother was also searching for a 'living Church' when he visited Taizé in 1963. 'To see if the reality corresponded with my mental image of it,' he said. In his heart he had already decided to join the community. He had first heard about Taizé in 1959, when he was on the editorial board of a student publication. Afterwards he collected more information and even wrote about it.

The brother, who came from a church-going family of the Dutch Reformed tradition, studied history and art history before going to France. During his student years especially he was constantly in search of a way to commit himself. 'I didn't want to be just a Sunday Christian; I wanted to give my whole self and all my talents,' he said. 'If the Gospel corresponds with reality, I thought, then it really *is* all or nothing.' He chose 'all', right in Taizé, because there he found a 'vision of Church renewal' and an 'anticipation of a more human world centred on the Resurrection of Christ'. He joined the community after making a retreat, returned to the Netherlands for a short time to finish – successfully – his doctoral exams, then, while continuing to study, devoted himself for the next five years in Taizé to working in the kitchen of the brothers' house, the pottery workshop, to learning about heating systems, making purchases in the market of Mâcon, and removing rubbish in the village. For someone who was on the way to becoming a professor's assistant and dreamed of writing a dissertation 'with lots and lots of footnotes', this was a totally new way of life. 'But it taught me much,' said the brother. 'I could have written that dissertation here, of course, but in the long run it was no longer necessary. I got over it.'

Since 1968 the Dutch brother has been involved with welcoming the young people, and so he has learned to know them close at hand. With reference to this he said: 'It may well be that here we don't offer the young people so much. Who knows, perhaps all those people come here looking for the same thing we are looking for. After all, in the church we all kneel facing the same direction.' And what about the Council of Youth, with its letters and visits, its tens of thousands of participants? 'We never tried to attract young people to Taizé in such large numbers. It grew, so to speak, after the youth meeting of 1966. Naturally, over the years we came to see it as a challenge.' But what could have awakened the interest of the young? 'I think that the trust the community showed in the younger generations in the late sixties had a lot to do with it. From 1968 on – the year of the student revolts in Paris – in France especially there existed a climate of discord between the generations. Hatred was everywhere: in families, at work, in public life. Young people were considered dangerous, destructive. Even in the Church, where they were accused of a lack of respect for bishops, and so forth. At that time of crisis and confusion Taizé stood up for the young. By pleading for understanding.'

Those days, however, lie far behind us. And young people still come in very large numbers to Taizé. Why? What motivates them? 'First of all, I think, because they find community here. The common prayer is probably the most characteristic element of it. How many agnostics gladly attend! I think they come because our community is one with Christ, and therefore universal. To the extent to which you seek Christ, all the barriers people set up are broken through. Christ has a particular plan for every human being. And then I think that young people are attracted to a place where struggle is not excluded from prayer. In the liturgy we pray for Bangladesh, for South Africa, for Russia. Very orthodox young people come here, as well as convinced Marxists. Because we ask no one about their political or religious beliefs. Once I asked a Maoist from Lyons exactly what he was looking for here. He answered: "Here I have the feeling I can be myself!"'

The Dutch brother is tall and wears glasses, and is blessed with a look that radiates youthful enthusiasm. In his presence one cannot avoid the impression that he judges his life above all by its beauty. What others call 'good' is 'beautiful' for him; what others find 'bad', he finds 'ugly'. For example he considers it beautiful that, in his experience, young people no longer view changes in structures as automatically leading to salvation, but want to be more open to human beings themselves. 'What really interests the young is the question: "What are you doing with your life? How are you dealing with the wounds you have received since birth, so that you become someone who is there for others?" Often such a question has to be answered before you can take on responsibility for the world. So that you become free of yourself, that you don't project your own problems on others.' And how do you do that? 'Contemplation is very important for this. Not as a kind of psychological hygiene, but an opening of the doors of your soul to God. And in so doing, growing in transparency towards yourself. For the Christian what counts is that man becomes himself in the presence of God. Anyone who tries to find political solutions and commits himself totally in that respect will have to commit himself totally in contemplation as well. In being silent before God.'

Is there room for this in the traditional Church? Isn't the silence often drowned in a flood of words? Doesn't the anonymity swallow up any sense of community? What do young people really think of their Church? 'For most young people the Church means a minister who preaches for an eternity, worship frozen into immutable forms – in short, an event in which they feel themselves outsiders. And also, the world of the Church has become the world of the middle class. If the Church were visibly poor, the poor in our society would find a place in it as well. I keep dreaming of a Church of the Beatitudes, a Church which looks for its security in Christ alone, and not in the consumer society, a Church in which everything is shared. In our congregations why don't we discuss how to make the profound vision of the first Christians, as described in Acts 2, 44, a reality in our time? Only if communion becomes authentic will something of it explode outwards to others.'

Is such a vision of the Church possible in our secularized

society, in which everyone maintains his or her own non-Christian forms of community? 'The question then becomes whether ways can be found to give meaning to being a part of the Church during the week as well,' suggested the Dutch brother. 'It seems to me that our urbanized society offers unique opportunities for people willing to meet, and so their mobility can serve a deeper purpose. Every Christian, with his or her particular gifts, should try to discover a way of serving in the Church. An enormous diversity of Church ministries would then have to be born, so that everyone could make the most of their gifts and use them to build up the Church.' Might Taizé be a prefiguration of such a Church? 'Taizé should not be imitated. What matters in the Church is the creativity of all. Renewal is possible here because the Spirit of God is active elsewhere, too, even if sometimes the action is hidden. There are enough places where God's plan for the Church is already becoming visible. Just look at countries like the Philippines, Zaire, Eastern Europe, where people try to be Christian despite the oppression and discrimination which that entails. Here in Taizé we are convinced that we are being supported by such Christians, that it is up to us to pass on the Gospel values they are living.'

'Will you, for love of Christ, consecrate yourself to him with all your being?' asks the prior in a loud, deep voice. The young brother facing him barely lets a second pass before answering. *Je le veux*; 'I will.' Silence. The two form the focal-point of some fifty monks in long white robes. It is Sunday morning in Taizé, and the church service is in progress. Some members of the young brother's family stand next to the prior. Even the organ is silent. 'Will you henceforth fulfil your service of God within our community, in communion with your brothers?' The brothers keep their eyes on their younger brother. 'I will,' he says again. Silence once more. Then, very slowly and solemnly, the promises of community of goods, celibacy, and accepting a ministry of com-

munion follow, like echoes of a rich past, like the spiritual relay
race of a universal Church, which has transmitted especially by her
monastic communities the message of the Resurrection, the promises of the Beatitudes, and the guarantee of the Sermon on the
Mount. Finally, at the end of the ceremony: 'Will you, always dis-
cerning Christ in your brothers, watch over them in good days and
bad, in suffering and in joy ?' It sounds like an authentic marriage
commitment, like an oath of faithfulness till death. 'I will.'

The profession has ended and the community is one full
brother richer. The Taizé Community numbers about sixty pro-
fessed brothers now, plus another twenty or so 'young brothers',
who have already entered but who still have to take their vows.
This is an impressive number, considering that monastic vocations have become fairly rare these days and that the community
has been in existence for less than forty years.

It is possible that the attraction of the community is due at least
in part to its international and ecumenical character. It includes
brothers from France, Switzerland, Great Britain, Belgium,
Holland, Sweden, Germany, Italy, Spain, Austria, Poland, the
United States, Canada, Indonesia, India, and Bangladesh. They
come from a number of different denominations, which are
strongly exposed to mutual influence inside the community. The
brothers come from Roman Catholic, Anglican, Lutheran, and
Reformed backgrounds and from different national traditions.
Practically all of them come from mainstream Churches as opposed to revival movements. The mutual influence of the different brothers' traditions resembles the physical process known as
'osmosis'. This implies less a discussion of justification by faith,
for example, than the cross-fertilization which is an inherent part
of living, praying, and working together.

The brothers vary in age from 19 to 66 years; the average age is
in the early thirties. The community sets neither a minimum nor a
maximum age for entry, but prefers future brothers to be on the
young side. Most of them are between 22 and 25 years old when
they commit themselves. Are such young men already able to make

such an important decision? A brother replies: 'Yes. Of course an element of risk remains, but that is built in, so to speak. What is important is that a vocation as such be recognized, that the one called puts what he has heard into practice. That obedience makes the uncertainty relative. If someone waited for total certainty, he wouldn't enter before he reached seventy, and even then he wouldn't have the certainty he desired. And then he would be giving only the "left-overs" of his life, while what matters is staking your existence as it is now.'

Someone wishing to enter the Community of Taizé usually begins by making a retreat for a week or two. This is a way of purifying his decision of inauthentic elements, by prayer and reflection – he might, for example, wish to escape from the world or from his personal problems. In this retreat he is accompanied by a brother, who finally discusses the next step with him. At the end of such a retreat, a man seldom enters immediately. He may return home for a while to say goodbye or to finish his studies. Often he first lives for several months or longer on the fringe of the community.

The entry is a simple ceremony, performed by the prior during an evening prayer. The new brother is clothed with the liturgical vestment – the white robe – and thereby becomes a 'young brother' (what traditional monasteries call a novice). He lives in the brothers' house, performs the tasks allotted to him, and is practically indistinguishable from the rest of the community. Taizé has not been afraid of entrusting important responsibilities to young brothers. For example, one of the brothers there was responsible for the finances of the community when he was still twenty years old. 'We really want to take seriously what animates the young people,' said an older brother. 'Often they need responsibilities more than we do, to test their commitment.'

Between the time of entry and the profession there is generally a period of about five years, sometimes more, sometimes less. The young brother already lives according to the promises, but he has not yet committed himself definitively to them. Weekly conversations take place with an older brother whose role it is to accompany him on his way. The reason for this is to help him to know himself, to become conscious of his weaknesses and possibilities, and to learn not to burden others with his difficulties. This 'introductory period' lasts till the young brother and the community have adapted enough to each other to make a permanent commitment to life together. During this time a young brother may change his mind and decide to leave the community.

'Will you, renouncing all ownership, live with your brothers not only in community of material goods but also in community of spiritual goods, striving for openness of heart?'

'I will.'

'Will you, in order to be more available to serve with your brothers, and in order to give yourself in undivided love to Christ, remain in celibacy?'

'I will.'

'Will you, so that we may be of one heart and one mind and so that the unity of our common service may be fully achieved, make your own the orientations taken in community and expressed by the prior?'

'I will.'

For the brothers of Taizé these three vows mean that, in the first place, they have no money at their disposal, except of course when they travel or make purchases for the community. 'When I need something,' said a brother, 'I discuss it with the brother who deals with financial matters. Together we figure out how much money I will need. Most of the time, though, a brother who needs money has already thought about how much would be adequate for him, in order to make the other's job easier.'

His job is not easy, since the community has never been well off. This is not surprising, as brothers who enter bring nothing with them. Gifts are not accepted – not even inheritances. The community has given up all its land, except the little plot of ground on which the house stands. And travel expenses, as well as the costs of corresponding with the quickly growing network of young people

throughout the world, are increasing all the time. Brother Roger explains: 'We began in Taizé with one house; now there is a whole complex of buildings. Bread is never lacking on our table. Every day we think about how we could live out the call to poverty. If community of goods were to lead to affluence, then the essential of our vocation would be endangered. To show clearly who we are, we have to refuse to place ourselves in a position of security for the future.' This attitude led, for example, to the plan to sell the few comfortable pieces of furniture which the brothers' house contained. Brother Roger talked about this plan in Calcutta, as he sat on a ramshackle bed in an unpainted little room where the noise was fit to wake the dead. But his voice was triumphant as he said, 'These people have even less than we do', and he indicated the impoverished inhabitants of the slum.

The promises made at profession pledge the brothers to a celibate existence. That needs no further explanation. But the question 'Why?' *does* require an answer. Why give up freely the little bit of human warmth still left in this materialistic, technological society of ours? An experienced brother says: 'What motivates all the brothers is the desire to use the life we have been given to serve God. To live no longer for yourself and your own interests, but for Christ. You can only commit yourself to celibacy if you believe with all your heart in the presence of Christ in your life, in the absolute reality of that presence; that Christ entered your life-history and continues to lead you day by day. In a very concrete way.' Don't you need an almost superhuman faith for this? 'Yes, but perhaps such faith is given to you in so far as you make yourself free and empty, and possess nothing and no one. To the extent to which you keep on burning your boats behind you. To that extent you give yourself over to the real presence of Christ.' Is that not possible if you marry? 'Marriage and celibacy are two vocations that cannot be separated. Theoretically you might be able to say that celibacy gives more scope for the universality of love, while in marriage you experience more the intensity of love. Two hands: one closed, the other open for many others. Together they form one image of the love of Christ.' But married love is not in itself a sacrifice. In giving you receive and in receiving you give. Whereas surely celibacy remains a sacrifice, even when you abandon yourself completely to your religious vocation. 'Every life in love means you have to leave something behind. Recognizing the other's existence means giving up a part of yourself. Celibacy also includes this dimension of dying to yourself – so as to live from and in Christ. But not a sacrifice in the sense of mutilation. Celibacy involves a struggle, an ongoing struggle that can take very painful forms. But it bears fruit too in the form of deep joy. It makes you capable of total love for the Other. Without such love celibacy is in fact nothing more than a sociological status, a burden that only makes you unhappy.'

The authority that the brothers of Taizé accept in their vows is represented by the figure of the prior. Not because of him as an individual, say the brothers, but because in him the solidarity, the communion, the unity of the community is made manifest. Accepting the ministry of communion exercised by the prior helps every brother to integrate his own creativity into the common endeavour. 'So, for example, I can't just say, "I feel like a holiday; tomorrow I'm going to Barcelona",' one brother said laconically. 'When I think I need a holiday, of course I can talk it over with the brother concerned. But most of the time you don't take the initiative for that yourself. When you feel like a holiday, the others often notice it before you do and they let *you* know.'

This might imply that the present prior, who is also the community's founder, is nothing more than this personalized solidarity. But Brother Roger is also the one who inspires the other brothers. In his absence no important decisions are made: the brothers telephone him or wait until he returns rather than take the initiative themselves. It is true that another brother is responsible for the continuity of the daily activities, but there is no hierarchy in the community. 'We don't want that,' a brother said. 'We don't consider the prior, either, as someone who stands at the head of the community, but rather at the centre, exercising a particular service there. Our conception of authority combines solidarity and autonomy.'

That the prior does not rule over the brothers in a feudal manner, but is rather the brotherly animator of the community, is illustrated by the fashion in which the community-family holds its meetings. Several times a week the brothers meet in the sacristy before or after prayer to discuss the events of the week. Sometimes those meetings last an hour, other times only five minutes. Once a year the brothers meet for an entire week 'in council'; for this meeting all the brothers who are able return from abroad, at least one per fraternity. Such a meeting is like a retreat, in which the past year is evaluated in relation to the community, the Council of Youth, and the universal Church.

The brothers' communion is most clearly expressed in their common prayers and meals. The latter took place for years in groups of seven, called 'foyers', into which the brothers were divided. Each 'foyer' had its own style: in some a brother read aloud during meals, while others were in complete silence or listened to music or held discussions. Since the autumn of 1976, when a number of brothers stayed in Calcutta, the community has been searching for other ways of eating together, especially ways in which visitors could be invited to join them.

Just as each brother has his own room, which he can arrange as he wishes, in the old country house or one of the neighbouring buildings, so too has each one another person inside the community in whom he can confide. Usually – but not always – this is one of the older brothers. For the rest of his life, trust and perseverance, joys and difficulties, and above all the search for God, are shared in this way. Such a trusting relationship is also important in the periods of difficulty which every brother experiences during his life. At such times the communion manifests itself most clearly. 'Knowing you are bound together in community life with one another until death makes you extremely sensitive to what the others are going through,' said an older brother. 'You only have to look at another brother's face to see how he is suffering. You can see it in the way he walks, the way he looks, his whole attitude.' Are there friends in the community who stand by him? 'In a community like ours there is a general climate of friendship. Any relationship which excludes others becomes a problem. Of course there are particular affinities, but they mustn't alienate you or cut you off from the others.' Aren't brothers in spiritual distress shown extra care and particular attention? 'Of course. But some difficulties can only be solved in silent communion with Christ. That's why it's important to leave room for discretion, too.' And in the case of inevitable differences of opinion? Do you sometimes disagree? 'Sure, but without breaking the communion.'

Besides the common prayer and the meals, the workshops of the community also serve as places of brotherly communion. Not for all the brothers, of course, since their work differs greatly and is not limited to the hill. Moreover, at any given time some twenty or so brothers are abroad. Since the brothers accept no gifts and a part of the community performs unsalaried work – such as helping with the Council of Youth or the welcome in general – the others must earn a living for the entire community. They do so in various ways. The community runs a miniature publishing firm, where some of the brothers work. Others work full or part-time in the ceramics workshop. This was begun by a brother who was originally a pastor, but who began to devote himself to making pottery shortly after coming to Taizé in the forties. Today his creations are displayed in museums all over the world, and he has a number of books on ceramics to his name. He is not the only artist among the brothers. There is also an organist, who has recorded a number of record albums, a painter whose stained-glass windows adorn numerous churches and cathedrals in Germany, Switzerland, and elsewhere, as well as the musicians, who take care of the liturgy. The community includes three doctors. One of them worked for a while at the Mâcon hospital, a short distance from the architect's office where yet another brother worked. Several brothers are engineers; one of them taught computer science in a technical high school in Cluny. Then there are the brothers who work in the co-operatives, those who devote their time to writing works of theology, those responsible for the upkeep of the house, those who do the shopping, and so on. Many of the brothers do both intellectual and manual work; most of the young brothers, for example, are responsible for receiving guests and at the same time performing household tasks and studying.

The same relationship between pastoral, social, and salaried work exists more or less in the fraternities in other countries, which as far as possible are financially independent from the brothers in Taizé. In Vitória, Brazil, for example, a brother-professor teaches sociology at the local university. The fraternities in Chittagong (Bangladesh) and Vitória together number from ten to fifteen brothers. For the most part, fraternities are only begun if an invitation to live a contemplative life among the poor has been received from the country concerned. Today, such a fraternity often includes young people who share the brothers' life. The brothers remain in a place for a certain time, leaving when others are able to continue their work. In the last few years the Taizé brothers have tried to start fraternities in every continent. For Africa a beginning was made in Cameroon, for Asia in the Philippines. Other settlements will undoubtedly follow. A practical disadvantage in setting up such fraternities is that often the brothers' radically Gospel-centred reputation has preceded them to a certain place. Because of their way of life and their experiences – especially with young people – the brothers are extremely sensitive to injustice. For example, this attitude was expressed concretely in work with trade unions and other forms of involvement against oppression and exploitation. As a result, the brothers have been accused of inciting working people and have had to leave the place where they were working. And brothers looking for work have been turned away because of this in places north-west of Taizé, where the brothers, who worked in the mines, were active in trade unions in Montceau-les-Mines. That the fraternity in Vitória can take such an active role in the diocese is due in part to the solidarity of Dom Luis Fernandez, the Roman Catholic bishop there, and to the diversity of the brothers' activities. One brother works as a deacon and catechist, another as a mason, while another sells newspapers and magazines: in his little van filled with magazines he drives through the town, engaging people in conversation and making contacts in the course of his work. Another brother, originally from California, began as a computer programmer, then studied theology in Lyons, and now makes stained-glass windows for churches. Then there are the brothers who remain at home to welcome guests and prepare the prayer. Such a fraternity penetrates society as in the Gospel parable of the leaven; it does not limit itself to a given class or social status, but proclaims the Risen Christ at the crossroads of society.

Aren't the brothers in the fraternities playing too explicit a role in the class struggle around them? A brother replied: 'We are in touch with many union officials and others who are deeply involved in social struggles. Giving up privileges is one of mankind's most difficult tasks. Over the years we have met so many people who struggle actively and whose authenticity we cannot doubt. As a community, however, we always look for ways of committing ourselves where we are required to pay the price. For example, we prefer to give concrete form to our solidarity with the oppressed by sharing their sufferings and thus becoming living signs of protest.' But often governments do not allow that. One has only to think of certain European, Asian, and Latin American countries where the Church has been muzzled. In such places the brothers travel as silent witnesses, without publicity, but with their ears and eyes wide open. Because 'only by listening to poor and suffering people can we give a new form to the Church'.

The community in Taizé loses no opportunity to let the brothers who travel speak out. Sometimes that takes place in small groups – when human life is in danger – at other times in the presence of young people and other guests.

Since it began, the Taizé Community has always emphasized the 'provisional' way in which it undertakes everything, and so inevitably the idea has arisen of transplanting the centre of the community to another country, or even to another continent. Over the years the community has received literally dozens of propositions for this. Again and again the brothers have decided against it, and not only for practical reasons. 'When you live so long in a certain region,' said a brother, 'you put down deep roots. And roots are important. A region stamps you in its own way.' Indeed, what would Taizé have become without Taizé?

*

You discern my thoughts from afar;
you know when I walk or lie down;
to you my ways are all known.
And words are not yet on my tongue
but you, Lord, know them completely.

'The 139th Psalm really means something to me; I discover it over and over again in my life,' says twenty-six-year-old Peter. 'Rationally speaking, of course, you could call everything it says into question. That every human being needs to be known by someone at a given moment, for example. But for me it has to do with faith, that I have been known, because that's what it says in the Bible. You are not just anybody, the Bible says over and over again, no, God knows you personally.'

Since May 1975 Peter has been living more or less permanently in the guest-house on the hill in Burgundy. He is one of the young people who introduce visitors to Taizé, lead discussions, and keep in touch with committed individuals and groups in other places. Peter is an engineer by profession; he studied road-engineering and hydraulics in Delft, Holland. Calvinist by background, he was active during his studies in the student chaplaincy, and there he heard about Taizé for the first time. He first came to Taizé at Easter 1972 with a group of his fellow students. 'There were 16,000 visitors and it was cold,' says Peter, looking back. 'At first I didn't like it at all – all those people, and that unusual liturgy. It was only during the midday prayer on Easter Monday that it hit me – the silence, the atmosphere, everything, really. I talked it over with one of the brothers and then I understood: it was all relevant to my own situation at home, to sharing together in simplicity and friendship.' Peter returned regularly to Taizé. After completing his doctoral exams in 1975 he decided to make himself available for an indefinite length of time for the Council of Youth.

I asked Peter and Alison, aged twenty-five, about their experiences of Christian community – here in Taizé, and also at home in Holland and Norwich, England, respectively. What does Christian community mean to Alison; what, in her opinion, are the qualities of that much-talked-of 'communion'? *Alison*: 'The kind of community in which people imitate Christ and stretch out their hands again and again to those on the edge of society, as Christ did to lepers, the lame and the blind, the woman caught in adultery. Community must not be based on a kind of easy optimism, an "everything'll be all right" feeling; no, it includes sharing suffering as well as joys. It is only Christian community if Christ really is a part of it, if each day we consciously place ourselves in the presence of God. In that way Christian community goes deeper than mere friendship.' *Peter*: 'When you feel that you are known by Christ and by others, you feel the need to be available for others too. Being in communion with Christ is not something individual, something you could do on a desert island. Community with Christ comes about in community with others, because Christ manifests himself in people of flesh and blood.'

The question arises as to whether Peter and Alison have found this kind of community in Taizé. *Peter*: 'For me it had already begun in Delft. Once I was asked to go and visit some people. I did so and I discovered then what an authentic personal contact can mean to someone. Christian community is based in the first place, I think, on really knowing real people, on building up good, that is, deep, relationships. For me Taizé was a continuation of that, and also a deepening. Here things are arranged in such a way that you are together with twenty or thirty other people for a week – living, discussing, praying with them in absolute cohesion. Within this structure, of course, community has to be created by the people

themselves – it's not automatic. The degree of mutual solidarity depends on how far the participants open themselves to each other. But the potential for authentic community certainly exists here.'

Alison: 'The first thing many people discover here is the value of common prayer. For me and many of us that was something restricted to priests and other clergy, until we experienced the services here and felt completely at ease. Another form of community here is the discussions, of course. What is especially important is the feeling that you are accepted just as you are, as well as the awareness that you all come from different cultures and yet are asking the same questions, searching for the same things.' And what are they? *Alison*: 'What it means to be a Christian. If that can be limited to going to church on Sunday. Every time I visit Taizé and then leave I think: how can I go further now?'

Alison got to know Taizé by accident when she was only fifteen years old. Her father, an Anglican clergyman in Norwich, accompanied a group of theology students to Taizé and at the same time made it into a kind of holiday trip for his wife and children. 'Taizé didn't impress me very much then. That happened only after I finished school, when I spent a year teaching in Cameroon. There I met a small group of young people from Taizé and what struck me was the way they put Christian community into practice. Their visits to other young people really made me think of the first Christians.' Back in Europe Alison spent a few weeks in Taizé, and after completing her studies of English at the University of Bristol she made herself totally available for the Council of Youth. In 1975 she spent nine months travelling in Africa; in 1976 she was one of the intercontinental team which wrote the Second Letter to the People of God in Calcutta with Brother Roger. How did she decide to become a full-time collaborator? 'I was present at the opening of the Council of Youth in 1974. There we thought a lot about the Council and I struggled with the question: can I see the Council apart from my own life-choices? I found the answer in a student group I had seen at work in Bristol, people who didn't view the Church as a hierarchy of structures, but as a community of human beings. Later I was reminded of this over and over again, during my travels in Africa, when I met people with very different commitments who nevertheless all had the feeling of belonging to something larger, something very concrete – a community experiencing the presence of Christ, I think.'

Many young people experience that Christian community for the first time in Taizé and, starting from that, try to give it concrete form in their local situations. Not so Alison and Peter: they came into contact with it in the cities where they studied – Bristol and Delft – and then experienced Taizé as the place where that community matured, thanks to the presence of the brothers and the international character of the hill in Burgundy. That raises a question: whether Christian community, such as that found in Taizé, can come to life fully in a local parish, a student organization, etc. A relevant question, it would seem, because brothers and young people in Taizé are continually pointing away from the hill to the universal Church which has to be renewed – by those who come to Taizé, among others.

Peter: 'A church building where an anonymous mass of 700 people comes together on Sunday is far from being a community. In order to be a community, first of all you have to know one another, and that's not possible with so many people. When you ask yourself what made the first groups of Christians communities, you find the answer, it seems to me, especially in the integration of praying, living, and working together. In our society that is not a realistic possibility for most people, but you can still take the essential elements and apply them throughout the week. By bringing prayer back into families, for example. Or by forming groups of not more than twenty persons who come together at least once a week to discuss the most important questions in their lives. Parents who discuss with one another how to bring up their children or unmarried people who talk about their lives. What is important is finding a common basis of trust, so that you can really be yourselves in the presence of the others. Something like that has to grow, of course; it takes one or two years. But the further you go the more you discover that you have a lot to say to one another.'

To what extent are people in this individualistic age ready to open their hearts to one another? *Peter*: 'I think it's different for every human being. Here in Taizé, where you eat, discuss, pray, make music, sing, and share a tent with others, and try to understand their lingo, contacts sometimes go very deep, but that's also because you know you'll never see each other again. I always try to make visitors aware of that by asking them: would you dare to say that at home? In the last few years, openness has been fostered at Taizé by asking people who take part in the group discussions to talk about who they are, what they do, and what their hopes are. It's very important that people learn to listen to one another. And to the Bible. Before, every now and then you would hear the criticism that the Bible didn't come up enough in discussion groups. Today that is certainly not the case.' Does Peter have the impression that much of what one experiences in Taizé is lived out in one's own parish or congregation? 'People come here who are very active in their own Church. People also come who are totally outside the Church and who can only refer to it critically. Sometimes the criticism is superficial and betrays a typical consumer-attitude. Like: the priest or pastor has to do everything, otherwise it's no good. Others take the initiative to create community themselves, but come up against resistance. It varies a great deal. In general you can find enough signs of hope to be optimistic. Small groups here and there. But history shows that it has often been such small groups which have been significant in the life of the Church.'

Alison agreed wholeheartedly: 'The parish I belonged to at home is that sort of community. The church attracts many visitors and we try very hard to give them the feeling that they are coming not only to visit a beautiful building, but to a welcoming community as well. Another church in Norwich offers a place to stay to people without a home. And in Bristol I know a parish where people are consciously trying to create deeper relationships among church-goers, in the political and social realms as well. Four or five years ago I would have said to visitors here: when you go home, try to

TAIZÉ

find like-minded people, form a little club and meet once a week. Now I say: look first at what is already going on in your parish or congregation, perhaps a living group that you can join already exists.' What does Alison feel is needed to bring authentic community into being, at home or elsewhere? 'To consider others just as important as yourself. When you are really convinced that we are all children of God, then that means that others are no less important, no less loved by God, than you are. And that means you have to use all your energy to tear down the walls of separation between you and your neighbours. That can succeed, however, only when you are ready to listen to others, to share their sufferings as well as their joys. Community has more to do with a frame of mind, a change in mentality, than with activities and organizations. No organization can make me open myself to others or others to me. That can only happen when we give up a part of ourselves. There are so many walls of separation in today's world. Couldn't the Church become a place where those walls are torn down?'

Undoubtedly. But it would seem to be easy to say that when you are in Taizé, where everything combines to give a young man or woman a deep feeling of solidarity: a week together, sleeping in tents in the presence of young people of the same age, under the influence of a beautiful liturgy. Evenings spent sitting around a bonfire. . . . Aren't there many more reasons in Taizé to speak easily and passionately about 'community' than there are at home? Alison considers this irrelevant: 'All kinds of reasons, I fully agree. But that doesn't matter. The fact is that here you can pray together, you can ask a young African, "What do you do? What are you looking for? What does being a Christian mean to you?" You can start a discussion with someone about their prayer and their life in a factory on Monday morning. All this helps you to discover others, it leads to a feeling of solidarity. Most people don't come here, I'm sure, to discover what the Church wants. Probably they visit Taizé because they want to be less isolated and talk with others, or because they can no longer find meaning in their lives. But by being here and participating they may begin to discover

128

something of that communion which is necessary for their own happiness, for the Church, for the world; that communion which is just as important as improving political and social structures. In any event young people come here for existential reasons. And for the same reasons Taizé directs them to their local church or to other communities at home.'

According to Alison, the Church cannot survive in human terms unless it once again becomes a community like the first Christian communities. 'And you can't be a community in big things, if you don't begin with little things.' And to do this we need the Church, to live the Spirit of Christ and to spread it. 'Because by yourself,' emphasizes Peter, 'you can never discover what Christ wants to convey in his Gospel. You have to discover that in and with others. So when people go home I always say: never think that you are alone.'

Although Taizé means more to many young people than Rome, Geneva, or Constantinople, it does not appear on most maps of France. Nevertheless, one can trace the route through Paris, Chalon-sur-Saône, and Cormatin. It is two in the afternoon and the bus from Chalon has just arrived. At the foot of the hill – a few miles north of Cluny – the travellers get out: from Scandinavia, Great Britain, Asia, the Netherlands, Belgium, and Germany. They swarm in and around the tiny railway station nearby, which today is only used for freight trains. From there the road curves steeply uphill, straight through the village. Here the passengers mingle with hitchhikers, motorists, cyclists, and hikers with back-packs. The higher one goes, the more the multi-coloured stream of people swells. Most vary in age from 18 to 25, and wear jeans and bright shirts. Some have the copper cross of Taizé around their necks; others are enveloped in plastic raincoats. All kinds of languages can be heard: French, English, German, Spanish, Dutch. . . . Some have evidently come far: they drag their feet, their eyes fixed on the picturesque medieval hamlet in front of them. The first thing that strikes you about the houses is that they are built of rough-hewn stone the colour of honey and are adorned with flowers. The village numbers only about a dozen such houses, which together form one short, narrow street.

To the right of the street, hidden behind large trees, lies an old country house which, with some neighbouring buildings, is the home of the brothers of the community. The house is bathed in the peace of a country village: it lies a safe distance from the centre of activity, and the brothers receive visitors there only occasionally. On the one hand this safeguards the contemplative character of the community, while on the other hand it leaves room for a certain autonomy for the young people on the hill. A corridor built by the brothers connects the house with a particularly elegant Romanesque church, which dates from the twelfth century. Until the Church of Reconciliation was built, the brothers used it for their common prayer; today it serves for the most part as a place of silence and meditation. In front of it is the village churchyard with the graves of the deceased brothers, Christophe and Philippe, and of Brother Roger's mother. Two houses, attractively set on the southern slope of the hill, serve as retreat-houses. They contain twenty-nine individual bedrooms and a dining-room. People spend a week there in silence; they don't even talk at meals. Each day everyone has a private conversation with a brother. Anyone who doesn't want to sit inside the whole day can take invigorating walks, or do a little work in the adjoining garden. A few hermitages are also sometimes available for the use of retreatants. For many people this week of silence and retreat is an experience which has a lasting effect.

The domain of the other Taizé-goers is limited to a square mile or so of land adjoining the village on both sides of the Taizé-Ameugny road. These grounds contain the Church of Reconciliation; the bells; the guest-house known as El Abiodh; the so-called Yellow House, where meetings with brothers take place and meals are prepared, a place of information and welcome; a *Salle d'Exposition* where pottery and other artwork is put on display and

sold along with books and records, all the results of the brothers' labours; large huts and army-surplus tents with thousands of rudimentary sleeping places; meadows complete with toilets and showers; parking places and other facilities such as a tiny non-profit store, a first-aid station, a telephone booth. The overall impression is that of an army camp occupied by a peace-loving troop of young folk, joyful yet peaceful, French yet international, crowded yet not congested. As one arrives one might see a few dozen people strolling calmly along the road, some lost in thought, others quietly talking. In front of one of the huts sits a group of Scandinavian and Germanic-looking people engaged in an intense debate. Beside the bells a young man wearing a beret is kissing his girl on the neck. A youth with Latin features is sitting by himself on the balcony of the Yellow House and strumming his guitar.

The welcome at the 'reception tent' is considerate. An English-speaking German, who introduces himself as Klaus, asks a sweating and panting group how many they are, where they come from, what brought them here, whether they speak any other languages. On their side the visitors also ask all kinds of questions, and so a conversation is struck up. It seems that there are different kinds of 'districts' where they can live corresponding with the way in which the visitors wish to spend the week. Some districts are for silence. Anyone choosing this spends his stay in Taizé in prayer and solitude, reflecting on his life and his commitments, alternated with a daily introduction by one of the brothers and possibly a private conversation. Then there are districts where thoughts, opinions, and information are shared about different aspects of the Council of Youth. The bulk of the discussion takes place in smaller, more flexible groups. Such districts are especially suitable for those visiting Taizé for the first time. A third category of districts consists of groups who spend their days doing practical work such as cooking, washing up, cleaning toilets, welcoming guests, and so on. The remaining categories consist likewise of groups that discuss, but those taking part in them go more deeply into certain topics

133

like centring your life on the living Christ, discovering signs of hope in your job or profession, seeking a new life-style in solidarity with poorer lands, and so forth. These so-called 'research districts' proceed along three lines: each of the participants introduces himself or herself starting from a question such as 'What priorities do I have in my personal life and my life in society?' Then there is Bible study and a discussion of the prospects offered in the Second Letter to the People of God, and finally meditation and discussion of the question 'How can I continue now that I have been challenged by the Bible and the Second Letter?' These groups are meant especially for people who have already been to Taizé and who want to go further in their commitment. In addition to these categories, in the last year or so brothers have begun leading meetings on the sources of faith. In these meetings, meant for people with no previous theological training, participants explore the essential elements of Christian faith; in presentations and discussions they touch upon topics such as the Resurrection, the history of Israel, the parables of Jesus, the life of the early Christians, and prayer and the sacraments. Everyone who visits Taizé is advised to stay for a week – from one weekend to the next, if possible. Those who bring their own tent can pitch it; all the others, that is the majority, are lodged in the huts and the army tents.

Every visitor is expected to choose one of these ways of spending the week, since Taizé is not a holiday resort. The guests are asked to help defray the expenses, since the Council of Youth has its own budget, separate from the community's, and accepts no gifts from organizations or Churches. That budget covers not only the cost of meals and the tents and other facilities, but also journeys made by young people from poor countries to share with many others the themes which have come up in the Council of Youth. The amount each visitor is asked to give is nevertheless a minimum; those who can give a bit more do so, and those who can pay nothing simply participate.

When the bell strikes three the discussions begin in the different districts. Groups form everywhere – in tents and huts as well as in the open air, on benches, or simply in a circle on the grass. Each district numbers twenty or thirty people, but for the discussions they are generally subdivided into groups of seven to ten people under the direction of a discussion-leader, or 'animator', as they are called. The entire Council of Youth is run by about 2000 animators who come from the four corners of the earth. They are young people who, at home as well as in earlier visits to Taizé, have already made a commitment and so can more easily help newcomers to begin thinking. Sometimes older people lend a hand: priests, ministers, lay people, including the elderly. The groups meet in the districts for discussions, Bible studies, informal conversations, and simply for being together from half past nine to half past eleven in the morning, three to five in the afternoon, and again at a quarter past nine in the evening.

On the grass near the bells sit a dozen or so Belgian, Dutch, and French youths. They are talking about the disappearance of hope everywhere: in the Church, at home, at work. Each one speaks his or her mother-tongue; the animator translates every French phrase immediately into Dutch, and a Belgian turns every Dutch phrase into French. 'You feel so helpless,' says Claude. 'Everything is already done for you. You have nothing to say. You just have to follow a road that is already mapped out.' Jan does not agree completely with that. 'You can vote if you want, be active in a political party, or begin something in your parish. You have all the power you care to assume.' The debate goes back and forth, interspersed with jokes and – sometimes – resounding laughter. The translations especially are often the cause of great hilarity. Everyone does not speak, of course, but those who don't are listening attentively.

Five o'clock is tea time. In the space of a few minutes long lines have formed at the kitchen. The sun has broken through the clouds convincingly and the crowd is now talking and laughing. Somewhere to the rear a group of Germans strike up a song. A brother is arguing with a French girl, one of the animators.

135

'Everyone is important,' he is saying. 'The heart is more important than techniques of organization.' 'That is nicely put,' she answers, 'but when there are more people in the tent than places to sleep....' The conversation is drowned out by loud laughter nearby as a chair collapses under a young Italian.

Shortly before half past seven the bells begin to ring and the crowd makes its way – slowly at first, then more quickly – to the Church of Reconciliation, sterile and grey outside, but warm and worshipful within. Dim light enters through a few stained-glass windows, while in front candles and tiny lamps create an exotic atmosphere. At the centre of the sanctuary stands a stone altar under a crown of candles. The church has in addition a simple lectern, an icon of the Virgin and Child, and, on the left wall, the organ. The nave is practically bare of furniture; only in the rear are there a few stools and chairs. Almost all the young church-goers are kneeling, bent low, or sitting with legs crossed on the carpeted floor. In this they follow the brothers, for whom a square in the middle is marked out on the floor with green twigs. The brothers enter the church through a small, adjoining sacristy, where they put on their simple white robes.

When the last, all-penetrating organ notes have died away, the crowd gathers outside in front of the church to greet one another and chat. Some of the brothers responsible for the visitors make appointments, while others accompany them to their tents or to El Abiodh, the house used by older guests, sick people, and others who are unable to stay in tents or huts.

As the crowd gradually disperses in front of the church, long lines form once again near the kitchen to wait for the evening meal. Jack, an Englishman, is twenty-eight and a social worker in London's East End. He is staying for two weeks at Taizé and is a leader of one of the research districts; his group consists of Englishmen, Americans, a Greek, a Frenchman, and a Dutchman. As they shuffle forward to receive soup from one person, an apple from another, potatoes and vegetables from a third, they discuss the experiences of the afternoon. In the research district the first meetings usually consist of the personal introductions of the participants, everyone in turn telling the group how his or her life has developed in relation to the chosen theme. That afternoon the Frenchman had blatantly idealized his very ambitious career in a doubtful public relations firm, following which an Englishman had announced that he was leaving the group. Jack said he regretted both attitudes. Personal introductions should be able to be frankly discussed. The Frenchman should learn to put his social success into perspective. 'When career or competition, the desire for a high salary or consumer-demands are your basic reasons for working, you are not far from exploiting others or being exploited yourself,' states the Second Letter to the People of God. That evening Jack would spend some time patching things up.

After the evening meal a group forms in front of the Yellow House to wait for the door to open at nine o'clock. A young brother telephones to the brothers' house to announce the arrival of expected guests. One after another, the brothers then stick their heads around the corner of the door, only to disappear afterwards into one of the parlours with a boy, a couple, or a group. Anyone wishing a personal conversation can also go to the church between five and six o'clock, where one or more brothers are always available. A much-consulted figure is Brother Roger, who in addition to a few hours in the daytime can be found almost every evening in the church.

Of the roughly 1500 visitors who populate Taizé during an average week in the summer, about 250 to 300 take part in research districts, 200 in group silence, 150 in the meetings on the sources of faith, 30 in personal retreats, 100 in the work group, and the rest in the discussion groups known as exchange districts. Every group has its own district, where the participants eat, sleep, and discuss. The exchange districts meet in the morning and the evening, while in the afternoon the participants have the opportunity to attend workshops on specialized subjects such as liturgy, politics, or the Council of Youth. There they meet members of other groups, and this serves to stimulate the work in one's own

group, which lasts the entire week. In the research districts the first day is spent in silence, during which everyone prepares their personal introduction. In these groups, moreover, a few hours of silence each day are planned.

Under a tree in a neighbouring cornfield sits a little group of people who look lost and disappointed. They have sheets of paper with mimeographed texts in English and Dutch in front of them, but they find the words too vague and too out of touch with real life. The animator, a serious German boy, tries to tell them they have to crack the text and try to find the thoughts behind the words. But it is too difficult for one young couple: tomorrow they will be going swimming at Cluny, they say. After a lot of talking back and forth, however, a discussion more or less gets going. About loneliness in European society. 'It's easier for people in Europe to go to bed with one another than to create genuine community,' says an English-speaking Italian. The discussion leader says that few topics are as popular in Taizé as solitude and loneliness.

Before they retire to their tents or huts most of the visitors take a walk on the hill. The dim light, the sultry air, and the rolling hills on the horizon combine to create an atmosphere of festive intimacy. Beside the bells, by the light of multi-coloured lamps, an impromptu guitar band plays an old English folk-song which a crowd of boys and girls are trying to dance to. On one of the parking-fields people are drinking wine by candlelight. A car coming from Ameugny with its headlights glaring is stopped and the driver admonished. 'This isn't Paris,' calls out a French teenager, sputtering with indignation.

In district 30 no one has gone to sleep yet, although midnight is approaching. The tent dwellers sit on the ground and talk about the paschal commitment. A Swedish girl explains in barely comprehensible English that for her faith is no hard-and-fast security, but a process of continuous searching and experimenting. A middle-aged man divulges that in his work people are really victims of others, but that he is unable to be a sign of contradiction without losing his job. What should he do? How should he put the justice of the Gospel into practice? One person suggests this, another that, until 'good night' is wished in at least five different languages. Tomorrow shortly before half past seven, the bells will ring again.

Twenty-three-year-old Johanna is from Berlin while Jorge, who is three years older, is from Argentina. They were helping in the reception at Taizé, though they were shortly to return to their respective homelands, Jorge as a conscript in the Argentinian army, Johanna as a student of Slavonic languages at the University of West Berlin. Both share a fervent desire for a better world, more equitable relationships among human beings, and a future of love. Such a future, they say, will not happen without a lot of struggle.

Johanna was seventeen when she first got to know Taizé; she was a member of a youth group led by a local parish priest. 'It was just at the time of my life when I had more or less rejected everything to do with the Church,' she said. 'But the church services in Taizé simply bowled me over. The intensity of the prayer, the singing, the silence – it was all new to me. Taizé wakened so much in me that I decided to come again two years later. Since that time I've been back every year.'

Jorge heard about Taizé for the first time during a visit to a Trappist monastery in Argentina. After completing his engineering studies he received a scholarship to study computer technology for a year in Eindhoven, Holland. From there it was easier to visit Taizé and in 1975 he spent Holy Week there. Since then he has been back several times.

What attracts committed strugglers for social justice like Johanna and Jorge to Taizé? The opportunity of dreaming up a better world by candlelight and guitar music? Or of really working for a more human future? But to do that should they be in Taizé, rather than in South America, Africa, or South Asia?

Johanna: 'There are enough political organizations in the world, but here I find a community of people who are trying, with their faith as the starting-point, to build such a world. They do it at home, each in his or her own situation, but they have come to Taizé to share ideas and to search together for ways of implementing them. There is a big gap in the Church between faith and prayer on the one hand, and social commitment on the other.' Does coming to Taizé help her and others to bridge that gap? 'I am firmly convinced of it. This past year I have been a member of a small community in Berlin. In it we have been trying to live as simply as possible, not as an end in itself, but to develop a life-style which will change the structures of our society. We share our income, pray together regularly, and open wide our doors to lonely people – often students, but others as well. The idea of living in that way with house and heart open is indissolubly linked with the search of the Council of Youth. We have also started a group for and with people affected by the job prohibitions. The Communists already had such a group, but it was for Communists only. Ours is open to everybody.' Do the official Churches co-operate? *Johanna*: 'At first they didn't understand us at all. It wasn't even possible to talk frankly about it with the local pastor. Only in the past six months has a change come about. To bring along the top when you start from the grass-roots is a very slow process.'

Jorge: 'Young people don't come to Taizé to change the world. I don't see Taizé as a breeding-ground for revolutionaries. People come here to reflect, to ask questions of themselves and others. In their daily lives most young people wrestle with an enormous tension between how they would like to live and how they really do live. Taizé enables them to talk about that and to discover all the different aspects of it.'

The question arises as to how those individual lives are related to the macro-structures of our society. Is it possible to change the latter thoroughly and permanently without actually sharing the lot of the poor, oppressed, and exploited?

Jorge: 'For me it is absolutely impossible to liberate other without taking their whole yoke on my own shoulders. Otherwise the liberation you are striving for gets bogged down in intellectual debating, for which the poor have no use. When I hear people talking about liberation in Europe, I often have to laugh out loud. Unless we stake our lives to achieve it, "liberation" is an empty and meaningless word. What good is it to poor countries if somebody spends half an hour demonstrating and the rest of the time doesn't give a damn?' Surely he doesn't mean that as many people as possible should go to poor countries to help out? 'Certainly not. Europeans have opportunities of their own. It is more than evident that the rich countries live off the poverty of the others. That can be changed only by a thorough transformation of mentalities. A new life-style is an essential precondition for such a changed mentality. By sharing the burdens of the poor, you can share as well the same hope and the same aspirations. Life-style and political structures cannot be separated from one another: they grow out of one and the same mentality.'

Johanna: 'In Germany we have the experience of socialism in neighbouring countries. And that experience demonstrates that when you only change structures, in reality nothing is changed. New structures must be informed by a new mentality. If you want to change structures, you should also be willing personally to pay the price. To the extent that we expect a more radical commitment by the Church, we have to move forward ourselves. In the little community I told you about, we tried to make that concrete by moving to a poor part of Berlin, where many immigrant workers live. That meant in practice for us giving up our privileges. Unfortunately most Churches – especially those in West Germany – have a great deal of difficulty about this. Many young people in my country have given up hope in the Churches because they are so rich and powerful.' *Jorge*: 'Most of our problems result from our power. Our first task must be to give up all forms of power. Simply be there powerlessly.'

But how can you create a better world without power? What will take its place? Love? But doesn't the (Marxist or capitalist) humanist appeal to love as well? To solidarity with others? What is so typically Christian about that?

Jorge: 'A humanist can also love very deeply, but that love can never be compared with the love Christ creates in us. Conversion to that love means that we feel with Christ's heart, see the world with his eyes, and listen to people with his ears. That love makes us transcend our human selves and gives an extra dimension to our Christian humanism. Only with that love can we find the courage to go on and on.'

'Christians for Socialism' see this love among other things at work in the class struggle. Johanna too? 'The class struggle is a social reality. There is no middle ground between solidarity either with the oppressors or with the oppressed. The Gospel asks us to range ourselves on the side of the oppressed. The language of the Beatitudes or the Magnificat is very clear about that! So in our struggle for the economic liberation of mankind, as Christians we will often find ourselves at the side of Marxists. But that doesn't mean in the least that we accept Marxism.' Does it mean accepting the methods of Marxism – revolution and violence? *Johanna*: 'The Christian's first answer is no. Even in the oppressor we recognize our brother whom we must love. But I don't feel myself capable of answering that question for a Latin American or a Filipino Christian. Ernesto Cardenal once said: God loves Samoza, but he doesn't love him as the dictator of Nicaragua. Rudi Dutschke thought that a Christian had to take part in the liberation from oppression as long as, in so doing, he still remained a Christian. . . . And so I think that the Church has to show clearly on whose side she stands, but at the same time she must not exclude anyone from her communion.'

What influence does Taizé have in this struggle against oppression, exploitation, and injustice?

Johanna: 'The Letters to the People of God, for example. They have been distributed in churches, but that in itself won't change anything. Taizé as a mouthpiece is in my opinion powerless unless each one of us lives out an anticipation of what those letters say.

In this the Council of Youth is an instrument of community; you can't get far alone!'

Jorge: 'The meaning of the meetings in Taizé for me is that people discover values which they put into practice at home. Of course preaching is necessary too, but the best kind of preaching, I think, is always doing what you believe in. And preferably together.'

In 1969 the question had already arisen on the hill as to whether brothers and young people should not keep in touch after the last of them had left Taizé and gone home, whether they shouldn't undertake a continuing search for a new face of the Church. This vision became a reality with the Council of Youth. Since 1970 young people cross the world to strengthen old contacts and make new ones, to visit other people inspired by this common adventure, each in their own country or continent. Many also make or continue contacts with others by letter, and so a correspondence to and from Taizé has come into being, from which a complete library of 'epistles' could be compiled. Like the apostles after the death of Jesus, they write to each other about life in their countries and developments in their communities, and they stimulate each other to prayer, love, and communion.

As a result one of the brothers in Chittagong wrote about the indescribable poverty – and the monstrous wealth – of the cities of Bangladesh. And a student from Central America told with undisguised suffering about the persecutions in that part of the world. 'I belong to a people which has to witness daily, powerless and suffering, how its children are dying,' he wrote in a letter to the community. A young man from Poland protested against greed and materialism, a mentality which subordinates *being* to *having*, and not only *having*, but *having more and more*.

How can young people in other countries, with other norms and structures, respond to all this? Groups in Berlin, Paris, London, and Vienna have each found their own answer. A girl from Paris wrote: 'In the neighbourhood where I live, all the doors are locked. Many different kinds of people live here: rich people, young prostitutes, drug addicts, poor old people, all unaware of each other's existence. . . . For three years now, a few of us have been meeting together for prayer and reflection on Scripture. As a result of this searching together and the bonds of friendship formed, I began to realize that I had to open my door. Now someone is always visiting: people who are lonely, lost, suicidal. Others who come to share their joy, to help out, or simply to exchange a few words.'

In this attempt to live a 'Christian presence' among the poorest of the earth, the brothers are ahead of the young. Their fraternities in ghettos and slums are silent witnesses to that. A brother from Chittagong, Bangladesh, described it this way in a letter: 'Chittagong is a port and the region is one of the world's most poverty-stricken. We have found a tiny place to stay on the roof of a newly completed building. The fact that we have a tap (frequently dry) is quite a luxury. We are living in a Muslim neighbourhood. One of us is spending a large amount of his time in building up contacts with non-Christians. Another brother is working as a doctor. He and three sisters are looking after one of the city's poor districts. I have regular encounters with students and other young people. Often you are overwhelmed by all the questions. Three times each day we come together in our bamboo chapel to pray, and that carries us along: contemplation, praise, and intercession. Often young people come to visit us. In prayer, conversations, or meals, we try to express and transmit our hope.'

It is in the letters of young people that their expectations for the Church are most apparent. Hélène from Lille writes: 'What the Church should do is ask for sacrifices from people. For me the solution is for every Christian to open his house and his heart to everybody. That's not easy. And it requires a long struggle. But it's the only solution. In today's Churches people are more than anonymous. They don't share, because they don't know one another. They are mutual strangers.' Or Agnes from Paderborn, who writes: 'I know that I am not alone, that there are people with whom I walk the same road. Together we are preparing ourselves for a commitment in the Church. Again and again we ask ourselves: how can the Church be the visible sign of the presence of God in the world? How can it be a universal community, a place of welcome for all? How can we become the people of the Beatitudes, in solidarity with the poor? The present situation in the Church seems threatening, but I think that it is only so to those with little faith. God never abandons his people.'

The festival begun in Taizé continues unceasingly. For most young people Taizé seems to be more than a few days' holiday, it seems to go deeper than a short-lived spiritual adventure, to reach further than Burgundy, France, or even Europe. 'What's important is that all over the world we create a network of people who radiate the spirit they have experienced here in their own situations. People who become the heart and soul of their parish or action-group, their trade union, in short, of the communities they belong to,' says Moiz from India. 'We don't want anyone to start "Taizé-groups". We would rather that the word Taizé be avoided as much as possible. We don't want to become a super-movement duplicating the work of others. It's much more important to infuse new life into local churches.'

And so the seed takes root. In Germany, Scandinavia, Great Britain, Spain, and Italy. In Asia, Africa, and America. In a Dutch boy who notes in his journal: 'After a successful trip home, accompanied by three Swedish boys and two Dutch girls, I am once again in the midst of everyday life, with the joys and the problems of work and study. Historically speaking, it seems as if a definite period in my life has come to an end. I am no longer in Taizé, I am no longer talking to people from all kinds of countries, I don't participate in the daily prayers. But I still notice every day that the joyful event that has begun is not over; that what I had hoped – and not only I – is true: the festival goes on. Even if it's not always so easy. So, for example, I have to hear, when I express my opinion (that an enterprise must exist above all to serve people and not so that my boss will have more money in his pocket), that I can't be talked to "as an equal". On the other hand, many others are interested in what has touched me. Besides my studies and my work I can find time now for prayer and meditation, to continue the adventure of inner silence. Pragmatically speaking, it's difficult to see what will happen now. It must, I think, happen in company with others who want to share in the festival too. . . .'

From the Writings
of Brother Roger

'If this rule were to be regarded as a final statement, dispensing us from always searching to discover more of God's plan, more of the love of Christ, more of the light of the Holy Spirit, we would be laying a useless burden on our shoulders: better then never to have written it.'

This is how Brother Roger concludes *La Règle de Taizé* (*The Rule of Taizé*, Les Presses de Taizé), which he wrote in the winter of 1952–3. As early as 1940 when he was alone in the house at Taizé, Roger had composed a booklet explaining his monastic ideal in some detail. By the early fifties, after the first brothers had made their life-commitments and the community was beginning to grow, they felt the need to express their ideals in a monastic rule. This was how the little book came to be written which deals with a life of joy, simplicity, and mercy; with prayer, meals, the council, and guests; with their commitments to celibacy, community of goods, and the acceptance of an authority.

That Brother Roger never regarded the Rule as the last word, but rather as the beginning of a long process of searching and discovery is evident from the series of books that he has written since then.

The first in the series, *Vivre l'aujourd'hui de Dieu* (*Today*), came out in 1959. It explains the ideals which led to the foundation of the community, and sets them against their theological and spiritual background. Its central theme is the universal Love offered to every human being, which sets him or her free to break through all the barriers between individuals and nations.

The next work in the series appeared in 1965 with the title
Dynamique du provisoire (*The Power of the Provisional*). In it
Brother Roger warns against obsolete Church structures which
continue to exist even when they lead to isolation instead of communication. He points to Christ and his disciples, who continually
found new ways of living in communion.

A year later, *Unanimité dans le pluralisme* (*Unanimity in Pluralism*) appeared, a book which widens and actualizes the Rule of
Taizé for people not living in a community. It explains, for example, why the brothers reject polemics as a means to ecumenism.

In 1968 *Violence des pacifiques* (*Violent for Peace*) was published.
It was written during the Paris student revolts in May and June of
that year, at a time when many young people were asking themselves if violence was essential in order to achieve a more just society. Brother Roger asks if a 'third way' exists which avoids the
pitfalls of both passivity and destructive violence, and he finds the
answer in the apparent contradiction of a peaceful violence that
appears in the Gospel.

During the preparation and the celebrations of the Council of
Youth, the prior published three volumes of passages from his
personal journal dealing with, respectively, the years 1969–70,
1970–2, and 1972–4. The first volume appeared in 1971 and was
entitled *Ta fête soit sans fin* (*Festival*, SPCK/Seabury, 1974). The
book tells of discussions with visitors to Taizé, a journey to Italy,
and how the idea of holding a Council of Youth came to Brother
Roger. The second volume was issued in 1973 with the title *Lutte
et contemplation* (*Struggle and Contemplation*, SPCK/Seabury,
1974). This deals with the struggle to give a voice to those con-
demned to silence, as well as with that other struggle which is
waged in the depths of our being, the place where no one person
resembles another. The third volume appeared in 1976 and was
entitled *Vivre l'inespéré* (*A Life We Never Dared Hope For*). In it
day-to-day observations alternate with recollections, accounts of
personal encounters, and meditations. Brother Roger speaks about
the life alive deep within us, which is so often extinguished by our

sense of impotence. He expresses his conviction that, to those willing to risk everything in faith, God offers a life exceeding all hopes.

The following passages have been selected from these books.

THE FESTIVAL OF THE BEATITUDES

If festivity were to vanish from people's lives . . .

If we were to wake up, one fine morning, in a society well organized, functional, and contented but devoid of all spontaneity . . .

If Christian prayer became an intellectual exercise, so secularized that it lost all sense of mystery and poetry, leaving no room for the prayer of gesture and posture, for intuition or emotion . . .

If the overburdened consciences of Christians made them decline the happiness offered by Him who seven times over declared 'Happy' on the Mount of the Beatitudes . . .

If those living in the Northern hemisphere, worn out by activities, were to lose the source of the spirit of festival, a festival still so alive in the hearts of the people of the Southern continents . . .

If festival disappeared from the Body of Christ, the Church, in all the world where could we find a place of communion for the whole of mankind?

*

If we are too concerned with the future we lose the day we have been given. Past and future uproot us from the present. We are off-centre.

It takes a great deal of courage to walk erect and unbowed as we advance towards Christ. To recover momentum, live the today of the Gospel and, with each new dawn, seize the coming day. Despair sets in only for the person left alone with himself.

Every age in life has its own special joy. By being sensitive to the pulse of the world and the Church – the world which is God's world too; and the Church, that meeting-place in the world of all

153

who confess Jesus as Lord – advancing age renews its youth from within.

Alive to what it is that fills us to overflowing, seek to discover, even in times of deep distress, the light in our darkness. The joy and the wonder at each new dawn of God.

*

Our existence as Christians means living continuously the paschal mystery: a succession of little deaths followed by the beginnings of a resurrection. That is the origin of our festival. From there every way lies open; our life can go forward, making use of what is good and of what is less than good. Festivity resurfaces even at times when we scarcely know what is happening to us, even in our hardest trial: a break in a deep relationship. The heart is broken but not hardened: it begins to live anew.

*

Do we realize fully enough that Christ never obliges anyone to love him? But he, the Living Christ, is standing at each one's side, poor and humble. He is there, even in our sorriest moments, when our life is at its most vulnerable. His love is a presence, not for a fleeting moment, but for ever. It is Eternity's love, opening a way of becoming, beyond ourselves. Without that elsewhere, without that way of becoming lying beyond us, we have no hope . . . and the urge to advance fades away.

*

The peace of Christ extends to the wounded regions of our being, to all that weighs us down and tears us apart, to the raw spots festering with contradictory sentiments, bitterness, images of an impossible love.

The peace of Christ requires time to soothe trials and sufferings. But now they no longer overflow; they are kept within oneself, and their hidden presence releases new energy.

No true peace is possible if we forget our neighbour. Every day we are confronted anew by the question: What have you done with your brother ? A peace which does not lead to communication, to fellowship with others, is illusory. At peace with himself, man is brought to his neighbour.

*

The spirit of mercy disposes the heart of stone to become a heart of flesh. It leads to a strong love, devoid of sentimentality, that caricature of tenderness. It refuses to turn the spotlight on oneself. It invites us to accept in quiet trust our neighbour, whoever he may be, and any event whatsoever.

And so our goodwill will extend to every human being, without exception, because in everyone we can perceive signs of Christ, our brother. Love your neighbour as yourself. We need a great deal of goodwill towards ourselves to realize God's kindness and love for us and, in our turn, to lavish kindness upon others.

*

Why is it that, although they say they know God, so many Christians behave as if they had never found him ? They show no mercy. They profess the God of Jesus Christ and yet their hearts remain hard.

On the other hand, why is it that so many agnostics, in the wake of the publicans and tax-collectors, 'are entering the Kingdom ahead of us', open up a way of peace, are men and women of communion, and show greater concern for peacemaking than many Christians do ?

There are many who profess to love Christ but do not know him. And there are many who love him, although they claim that they do not know him.

*

Only someone with a sense of continuity can benefit from the dynamic of the provisional. Enthusiasm, zest, is a positive force, but it is by no means enough. It burns itself out and vanishes if it

155

does not transmit its emphasis to another force, less perceptible and lying deeper within, which enables us to keep on our whole life through. It is absolutely essential to ensure continuity, for every life has its periods of monotonous travel across arid deserts. The interplay of these periods is a source of refreshment.

Perseverance is the continuity of Christ throughout the dull days of life – one of the main lines of force around which the Christian life is fashioned. This road to Christ is always the most precarious.

*

Very often, whatever we may think, our ordeals, failures, and standstills constitute a driving force stimulating us to create, to such an extent that the impossible opens the way towards the possible.

*

We may achieve marvels, but only those will really count which result from Christ's merciful love alive within us. In the evening of life we shall be judged on love, the love we allow gradually to grow and spread into merciful kindness towards every person alive, in the Church and throughout the entire world.

*

Nothing is disastrous, except the loss of love.

Discovering a living relationship with God . . . contemplating him in the faces of others . . . restoring a human face to those disfigured . . . all of that is a single struggle, the struggle of love. Without love, what is the good of believing? Or of going so far as to give our bodies to the flames?

No, as we struggle nothing is really disastrous, except the loss of love.

TAIZÉ

THE GATES LEADING TO GOD ARE CALLED PRAISE

At the present time, no Christian can afford to lag behind in the rearguard of mankind, where there is so much useless strife. He must at all costs avoid becoming bogged down.

In the struggle for the voice of the voiceless to be heard, for the liberation of every person, the Christian takes his place in the very front lines.

And at the same time the Christian, even though he be plunged in God's silence, senses an underlying truth: this struggle for and with others finds its source in another struggle that is etched more and more into his deepest self, at that point where no two people are quite alike. There he touches the gates of contemplation.

Struggle, contemplation: two poles between which we are somehow to situate our whole existence?

*

Prayer is first of all waiting. It is allowing the 'Come, Lord!' of the Apocalypse to well up in oneself day after day. Come for mankind! Come for us all! Come for me!

It is not the privilege of a few. It is an easily accessible reality, for tiny children as for the old. It finds expression in innumerable ways.

Insofar as prayer remains the expectation of Him who is not I, it is neither flight nor projection of myself. There comes the moment when I can only say: you are the other, you are he who exists as himself.

In the encounter with this Other, our intentions are purified, our hearts become transparent. Before this Christ who exists in himself, who could keep up any pretence?

*

One intense conviction: any communication with God leads us towards our neighbour. The sign which proves the authenticity of our inner life – of our relationship with Jesus Christ – is how attentive we are to others. If our neighbours vanish from our dialogue with Christ, then our love for God has more to do with some mythical deity completely detached from human concerns than with the Christ of the Gospel. In those without God, love devours the soul, in Christians the soul suffocates if love of God precludes love for others.

*

Faith means believing without seeing. It is not afraid of the dark, nor of the dark regions of the personality. It is certainty. It allows us to go forward in spite of thick darkness.

In one sense, prayer is a step from doubt towards faith, a creative waiting to perceive in every event the Creator at work today. It is secret wonder and thankfulness for the gift of life.

*

Our inner life must be a driving force for our entire being – body, soul, and mind. Watchfulness should never be limited only to our thoughts or to our body. The physical and the psychical are so closely related and interdependent that any disorder in one brings about a disorder in the other.

Spirit and body are one. To keep them open and available for God to act is the basis of our whole inner combat. The aim is to maintain the creature in a constant communion with his Creator. With one purpose in view: the lordship of Christ Jesus over our entire being.

*

To want a life with no contradictions, shocks, opposition, with no criticism, is to fall into disincarnate dreaming. Confronted by the shaking of foundations, in ourselves, in the Church, or in human society, we are offered two ways:

Either hurt and anguish pass into bitterness, when, groaning under the crushing load, we become rooted to the spot and all is lost.

Or else pain and sadness find an outlet in the praise of His love, lifting us out of passivity and enabling us to deal with anything that comes our way.

LIVING CHRIST FOR OTHERS

In this period of human history when every person is so unprotected, at the mercy of images, ideas, and the media, the option between mediocrity and sainthood has never been more clear-cut. The lukewarm exclude themselves; they are unfit to take a stand and to renew from within the social group of which they form a part.

Out of the depth of human distress there rises an appeal. In our everyday life and work we are ordinary people, the extraordinary lies hidden. The world needs people who are outstanding more by their loving concern than by their natural qualities.

*

Christians are not entitled to opt out of the world's tensions, but neither are they entitled to surrender to the impassioned attitudes which those tensions provoke. More than ever they are called to be people of peace. How else can they be 'in the world but not of the world'? When our hearts are at peace before God, we will help others to forget their fear, the source of hatred and wars.

*

Would a Christian be afraid of dirtying his hands by participating in the betterment of mankind and the creation of peace on earth? Pietism is to be feared when it prohibits all involvement in economics, politics, and the human sciences.

In the years to come, one of the characteristics of genuine Christianity will be its ability to prepare new kinds of relationships among men. This would be political commitment in the widest sense of the word: not partisan struggle, when horizons become narrower and when everyone runs the risk of serving the interests of a faction, but the building of the city of man.

All of us are challenged by the necessity of sharing. This cannot be limited to a restricted area, to one local or national community. In the renewed awareness of the needs of people throughout the world, Christians will be required more and more to see themselves as part of all humanity. That is our vocation to catholicity, to universality.

*

If Christians want to show that they are serious about creating communion among all men, they must begin by searching for ways of promoting a just distribution of the products of this earth. The countries most densely populated by Christians possess tremendous wealth in comparison with non-Christian countries, devoid of material resources. This is a fact. In the middle of this century, for example, the standard of living in the United States was thirty-five times higher than in India. How this enormous problem is handled may well determine the future of Christianity.

*

The creative and artistic capacities of the people of the Southern hemisphere represent an active force which could come to the rescue of the intellectual atrophy of Northern countries. Every segregation of South from North means a slow death for the whole of humanity. The complementarity of cultures is the future awaiting us all. The interchange which will take place between the intuitive gifts of the one and the analytical gifts of the other is a creative force.

Will the West be able to compensate for its difficulty in entering into authentic human communion by opening itself to the spontaneity of Africans in particular ? Will our individualism, reinforced

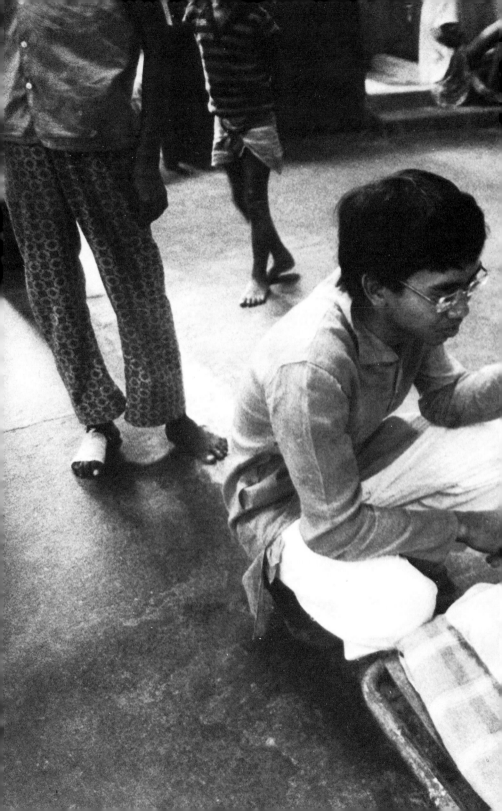

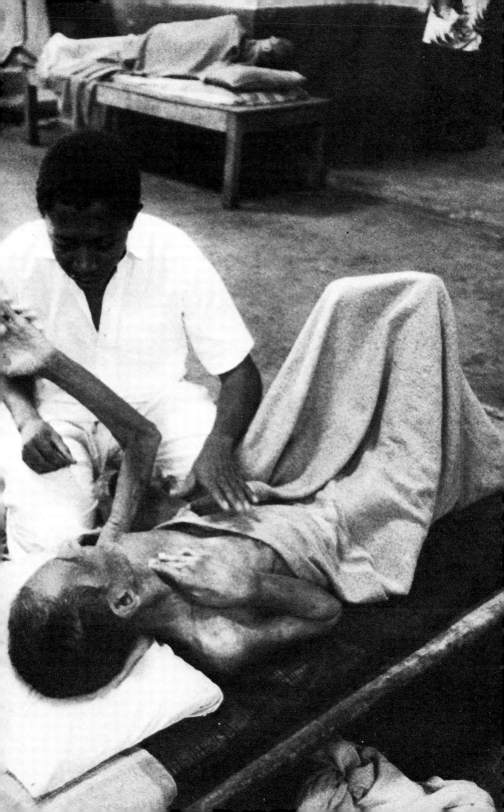

as it is by an affluent civilization, discover by contact with the Southern nations an ability to share?

*

Every one of us, Christian or not, has violence in his make-up. The only difference lies in the way we use it.

Among Christians, two contradictory attitudes!

For some, violence is repressed and leads to a flight from reality. The result is pietistic passivity and an absence of all commitment on behalf of those suffering injustice. Prayer is enough. Anything else would mean risking dirty hands.

At the other extreme are Christians who want violence or even, if it is effective, armed force. They see no other way of registering their protest against the oppression of the poor by the powerful, especially when the oppressors employ a disguised violence.

Could there be a third way, between passivity and destructive violence? Did not Christ say that only the violent take possession of the Kingdom? The Gospel spews out the lukewarm, only those on fire can enter!

Everyone has to discover this road for himself. Violence for Christ adapts itself to the age and the context of each life. The way cannot be laid down in advance.

*

No one is built naturally for living the radicalism of the Gospel. In every person the yes and the no are superimposed.

Yet it is through giving himself globally that a person grows. If he risks his whole life, that becomes the preparation for events beyond his wildest hopes. Situations of standstill, discouragement, or fierce struggle, far from demolishing, build him up. What most threatens him is transformed into a means of lightening his heaviness.

The moment comes when we receive what we no longer even expected. What we had never dared to hope for arises. A gleam of Christ in us. Others see it shining, although we may be unaware of it. Nothing is to be gained by knowing what light we reflect; many people already reflect God's brightness without knowing it, perhaps even without daring to believe it.

For those who risk their whole lives, no road ever comes to a dead end.

A PASSION FOR UNITY

The coming generations will have less and less patience with the contradiction of Christians split up into different denominations, with all the energy lost defending opposing viewpoints, at a time when the population explosion is rapidly increasing the number of people with no knowledge of God. They will find it intolerable that the best of Christians' time and energy is going to waste justifying their respective positions.

*

Since the fourth century, few can have been more decisive than our own. Either modern Christianity will rise to one of the main challenges of the Gospel, the sense of the universal, or else the Christian Churches will turn in upon themselves in those parts of the world where they have taken root, and so obstruct the flow of 'grace, source of salvation for all men'.

*

Many of the young love Christ in isolation, without his Body the Church. In their thinking, the Church has often already been replaced by a political universalism. I should worry little about that, were it not for the last prayer of Christ before his death: he asks that, just as he is in communion with his Father, a demanding communion of the same nature should exist between his followers. He has this final intuition: the credibility of Christians passes by way of the communion which binds them in a single body.

If Christians seek to be visibly in communion, this is not an end in itself, for a greater sense of ease or for greater power, but so that others may see the truth in them, in order to offer to all men a place of communion where even non-believers feel at ease, under no kind of constraint.

So I have never better understood what is at stake in the Church, and what lies at stake in its rejection, or in those underlying struggles which are current in it.

Our communion, a fire kindled over the whole earth, burns within us.

*

Every change in human nature works from within. It is from within that our intellectual structures are modified. It is in the intimate places of the heart that continuous conversion to Christ takes place – the Christ we are continually forgetting, and continually denying.

Of course we must do all in our power to reform antiquated structures. If such structures are not animated by men of generous heart, however, reforms make them look better, they will have the merit of logical consistency, but they will shed no light.

*

It may be necessary to react to the dead weight of a Christian community. But if those who express themselves in this way become protestors and if, moreover, they regroup and clamour from outside, they hold back the Christian community, exhausted as it is by its long journey, and they hinder its rebirth. How to be capable of being leaven in the dough, raising it and cracking the crust which always forms and re-forms over ageing institutions ? Nothing can resist such leaven.

*

Passion for communion in the Body of Christ, his Church, entitles no one to ride roughshod over the people of God in its slow progress. Anyone who would plunge the great mass of Christians into hopelessness in that way would be heartless. Very often it is childlike faith which has been passed on to them. Is anybody entitled to tie a stone around the neck of the simplest member of God's people, and so to wound the body of Christ himself?

There are those sturdy enough to stand at the forefront of the Church's life; they take the risks and prepare the way forward. Already, all over the world, Christians are becoming brothers and sisters of non-believers; that is one of the clear signs of our times. Christians everywhere are becoming more and more aware that they are part of the whole human community, and are called to be leaven of unity in a secularized world.

Keep within the body of the whole people of God, stay at the Church's front lines: there is no contradiction in those two aims.

*

Who is more attentive to his neighbour than a man or woman who is truly Catholic? Everything is able to enter into their secret hearts: concern for every human situation, the prayer of the Church throughout the ages and its contemporary realization, tears for someone in trouble and joy for someone thankful for today. They are capable of a passionate concern for unity, no matter what the cost: not in dreams but in existing Churches which, by a law of sociology, are always tempted to put the local situation first, and thus slow down the dynamic of catholicity.

*

Why such discord among Christians?

O Church of Christ, are you becoming a secularized locus of spiritual debility, a colourless centre of conformity to worldly fashions, devoid of all signs of meeting with the Risen Christ – salt without savour?

Are you becoming a frozen, stereotyped image of the Christian community, a place where people are no longer challenged to take a bold, demanding leap beyond their limitations, an act which would convey to others in the human family their confident expectation of God's coming, and assure them of the certainty of a presence, the Risen Christ?

Are you becoming a place where people are incapable of welcoming others, communicating Christ to modern man, and living the Gospel in all its freshness?

Are you becoming a mere collection of splinter-groups, a place where pluralism turns into fragmentation or simple co-existence? If pluralism runs counter to unanimity, will Christ still find faith upon the earth?

PARABLE OF COMMUNITY

In living a common life have we any other aim than to unite men committed to following Christ into a living sign of the unity of the Church?

A few men, living in isolation, could not accomplish much, but the same men, united in a common life, can stand firm in a faith capable of moving mountains: they are enriched by that quality of Church life inscribed within every community which is bent on maintaining the authenticity of its vocation.

A community is a microcosm of the Church, it recapitulates within itself the full reality of the Church. And so the humble sign of a community can resonate far beyond the limitations of the men who compose it. Yet we have no desire to start a school of thought in theology, literature, or in the human sciences. Building up a following means nothing at all nowadays.

*

Does not the burning thirst for human relationships have its source in the presentiment of another and more essential communion, our relationship with Christ?

More than ever, the younger generations are set on communicating. Are they not ripe to consider that, beyond the limitations of all human intimacy, at a given moment One alone can fill our solitude?

A close life-long friendship is not given to everybody. But a time of richness, an experience of friendship limited in duration, can leave its mark upon a whole lifetime. It wakens energies hitherto unknown. It transforms the core of the personality, making it more human and welcoming.

*

More than ideas, the world today needs images. No idea is credible unless it is clothed in visible realities, otherwise it is only ideology. A sign, however weak, takes on its full value when it is something from real life.

*

By its very nature, community life turns towards both God and men. If it favoured purity of life alone, it would be in danger of dying a slow death. It calls for the capacity to adapt to renewals.

Being too far ahead of one's time leads to debility and fruitless argumentation. But lagging behind destroys the momentum of a life given for others.

Today more than ever, when it is charged with the life-force proper to it, when it is filled with the freshness of brotherly love which is its distinctive feature, community life is like yeast at work in the dough. It contains explosive power. It can raise mountains of apathy and bring to men an irreplaceable quality of the presence of Christ.

Very often, in the darkest periods of history, a small number of women and men, spread across the world, were able to turn the course of historical developments because they hoped against all hope. What was doomed to disintegration entered instead into the current of a new dynamism.

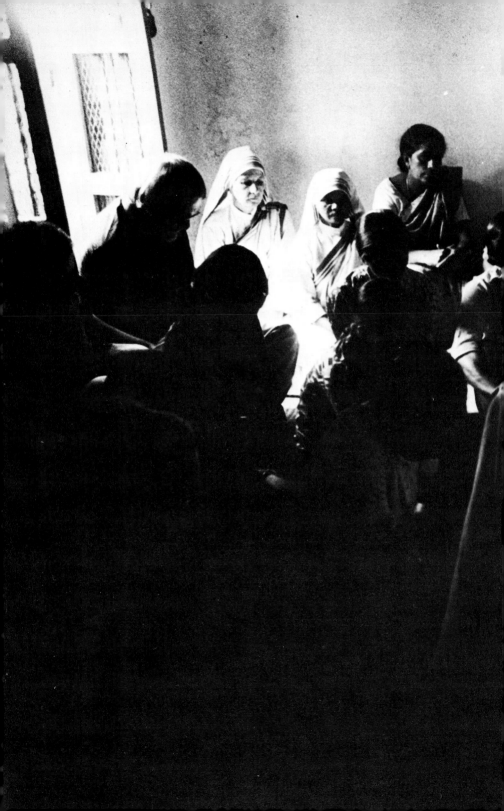

OVERFLOWING WITH HOPE

To become a ferment of communion in the world, the means at our disposal seem very slight. The yeast and the dough look so much alike that our eyes strain to see the difference. Yet invisibly the yeast contains the power to transform everything. Everything is hidden within it, and therefore the infinite becomes possible.

Yeast must always be well mingled with the dough. And each of us must be present at the heart of the Church and of the world, with that discreet presence characteristic of every life hidden with Christ in God.

*

Could the call to reconciliation ever invite passivity or life without struggle? No, the Gospel has never led to tranquillity. Being reconciled with oneself, as with others, supposes a readiness to accept tensions and struggles. By neutralizing or fleeing situations of crisis, vital energy is destroyed. Passing through crises, looking beyond . . . is a road that takes us far.

*

Man is created for hope. For him all things are continually being made new.

One day, at the heart of our darkness, a living word lights up. Irresistibly, it opens the way to other men.

Christ does not force anyone to follow him.

The Gospel is not a system, a vice to grip other people's consciences and our own. The Gospel is communion.

In Christ, God made himself poor and hidden. A sign of God cannot be an image which overpowers. God does not ask us to work wonders beyond our means, he wants us simply to understand how to love our brothers.

In these years we can sense a new birth: the People of God on the march towards communion. Prophecy is not dead. Beyond the violence of the present, a new hope is rising.

*

If the older generations have no right to impose themselves to the exclusion of others, neither can the young take advantage of their age. The Christian community is not a copy of civil societies; everybody has their contribution to make. The generation gap goes against the spirit of ecumenism, and each of the generations risks losing everything: the young because they no longer benefit from the human and spiritual experience their elders have acquired, the not-so-young and the elderly because they are relegated to a situation where they have no life to live, and can only wait passively for their own deaths.

*

The futility of my life: this is the cry welling up from the depths of most people.

Who really believes that his life has achieved anything? And who could claim to be totally useful? Even at the peak of a fulfilled life we remain poor servants but, at the same time, we are co-workers with God. There is nothing contradictory in the dialectic of the Gospel. Those who sow in tears of futility harvest in song. One day brings flowers, and the heart rejoices. Then the flower falls and there follows the season of waiting, the season of the fruit. An entire lifetime is barely enough for it all.

*

Once again I hear a familiar question: How can I be myself? How can I fulfil myself? Those questions preoccupy some people to the point of anguish.

If 'being oneself' means dropping our masks, giving up conformist attitudes and conventions, who would disagree? That is not just good, it is vital.

173

Yet when the Gospel asks people to be themselves and develop their gifts and talents a hundredfold, it is not in order to serve their own ends, it is to serve others.

In the Gospel, to be oneself means searching deeply until the irreplaceable gift given to each one of us is revealed. Through that special gift, unlike anyone else's, each person is brought to fulfilment in God.

So keep silence, withdraw into the desert, if only once in a lifetime, and discover that gift. . . .

*

One question has kept coming up this summer: 'How are we to continue after leaving Taizé?' And I would answer: Nobody can possibly grasp all there is in the Gospel. But if during your stay here you have understood just one word – almost nothing – then put that word, that gesture, into your life, at once and intensively. When you have put one foot forward, that step will lead you to other steps. Put into life the little that we have understood, and create starting from that tiny intuition, starting from our own poverty. Strive to find just one intuition and then to live by it.

*

Beyond the tremendous open confrontations now going on, the Church of tomorrow is being born. A springtime, at our door.

Every new birth is accomplished in patient suffering. But with the support of so many young Christians, how could we not be overflowing with hope?

Our hope is Christ within us. The more we allow ourselves to be inhabited by this reality, the more we can stand firm against wind and tides.

There lies hope. It keeps our heads above water, and comes to bring joy to our hearts the very moment doubts arise. It lets us see God, present beyond our inability to believe to the full.

*

Wait! Wait for the dawn of a life, when God gathers us to Himself for ever. Wait for the springtime of the Church. Wait, in spite of everything, for Christ to transfigure our failures and turn our bitterness into the spirit of mercy, for love which is not consuming fire is not charity.

God is preparing for us a new Pentecost which will set every one of us ablaze with the fire of his love.

The Holy Spirit, always unsettling, is stirring up his people. He is making them capable of encountering all men, and together running to meet the event which will upset all our human calculations and bring life to our dry bones.

Run towards, not away! Run towards mankind's tomorrow, a technological civilization charged with the promise of human development for the poorest.

Run forward to bring new life from within, asking people, exhorting, imploring them, in season and out of season, to come together, and so to raise up in the world of men an unmistakable sign of our brotherly love.

A Conversation
with Brother Roger

Brother Roger, when did you first feel that God was calling you to give your whole life to him?

One of the most significant events of my life, I think, was when I was a little child, at the end of the First World War. My grandmother arrived from France. Up to the time the bombs were falling round her home she had taken in fugitives: pregnant women, children, old people. Then, when she was compelled to flee before the advancing German armies, she left for the South of France. At a time when her three sons, Frenchmen, were fighting the Germans, and Europeans were at each other's throats, suddenly she could bear the divisions among Christians no longer. She was a member of a family which had been Protestant for more than four centuries, and she decided to receive Communion at the Catholic church. About a year later she arrived at my parents' house. Her actions had a deep and irreversible effect on me.

What affected you so much?

The fact that she had the courage to share the lot of those who were suffering most. And also her unexpected gesture: when she could no longer stand the intolerable disunity in Europe, she felt intuitively that the Catholic Mass represented something essential. This intuition of hers left a deep impression on me. I will bear its stamp till my dying day; while I was still a child, it gave me a Catholic soul.

So your vocation was ecumenical from the very beginning?

Certainly. And, in 1940, when I began offering hospitality in Taizé to political refugees, I was unconsciously imitating her gesture.

After that childhood shock, how did your vocation gradually take shape?

When I was still young, I acquired a strong conviction that it was essential to discover a few guidelines to refer to throughout my life, if I was to accomplish anything that would last. I was about eighteen when I became convinced that a person could only grow and be integrated by developing from his chosen lines of force. Without these essential and permanent reference points, nothing strong and enduring could be created in life.

What were these reference points?

They form our original rule, the one which was never published. They appear throughout the *Rule of Taizé*. Particularly the words: throughout your day let everything be quickened from within by the life of God.

Does that mean that, when you were still very young, you already wanted to follow Christ personally?

Of course.

What was it in Jesus Christ that fascinated you?

His compassion. His ability to love and to understand.

Do you think that your grandmother's behaviour influenced your own attitude towards the Church later on?

After the effect which my grandmother's decisions had on me, my parents sent me, when I was thirteen years old, to board with a Catholic family. That increased my consternation: how was it possible that these two families, my own and the one I stayed with, could be divided in faith when on both sides there was so much honesty with God?

So you recognized in these Catholics brothers and sisters of yours?

Certainly. When I was still a child I would go into a Catholic church to pray. I had seen my father go in. . . .

Your family played a very important part in your life, didn't they?

That's true.

Are you thankful for that?

Yes, though even when I was young, I felt rather apart from my family. I was born after seven girls. The youngest was musical. Even when she was little she played the piano constantly. So I was always sent out to the garden.

Were you always on your own?

By force of circumstance I was alone in the garden. And yet there were nine of us children, and there were always lots of people at home, lots of guests.

Did you have an unhappy childhood?

I had a beautiful childhood. I didn't particularly want anyone to be concerned about me. Life in the garden was poetic. I loved to follow the seasons. It was probably my sisters who made me aware of the beauty of it all. One day, I must have been about a year old, I was forgotten and left outside in the garden. At midnight my mother remembered me. They had forgotten all about me, but I was sound asleep in my chair. My adolescence was more difficult because my father was going through a difficult time and I was involved in it too.

What was the difficulty?

It concerned the Church, but I never talk about it to anyone. I can't bear to slight his memory. But I thought my father was worrying about things of no importance and my mother thought so too: because of a confident attitude towards life which we both shared, we were perhaps inclined to make too little of his sufferings.

When and how did you resolve to live according to the monastic commitments you made later?

It's almost impossible for me to know when that idea came to me. But I do know that on at least three or four occasions I considered doing something else: being a writer while living as a farmer. But I always realized straightaway that my life would have to be both extremely demanding and something to which God would call me.

When and how did it happen?

On my mother's work-table stood a picture of Mother Angélique Arnaud, of Port Royal, in her monastic habit. I knew that she had been courageous like my grandmother. And speaking of her my mother would say, 'She's my invisible friend'. One day, at Port Royal, Mother Angélique decided to upset the easy life of the women with whom she lived and to transform their community life completely. I learned about that when I was eleven or twelve, when my mother used to read aloud to her seven daughters. Every day we would all go and be read to, and we returned again and again to the beginnings of the reform of Port Royal. It wasn't Jansenism that interested us, but the community life lived by those few women.

So they are behind what you are living today?

Theirs was the only example of community life I had. I had no other image of it when I was a child. It was only much later that I visited a Charterhouse. There I found something that corresponded to a certain extent to the demanding way of life I had glimpsed, and I made two or three retreats there.

And later you were to introduce a similar monastic life within the Reformation. . . .

I never wanted to be part of a process of 'restoration' of the monastic life. I have never believed in such a process. Nor did I ever want simply to integrate monastic life into the Churches of the Reformation: that would have merely consolidated the parallelism between denominations which blocks communion among Christians to such an extent. What I am passionately seeking, I believe, is something very concrete: a parable of communion incarnate in the lives of a few men, for words have no credibility until they are lived out. I was haunted by the idea: why not put into the dough of the divided Churches, indeed *all* the Churches, a leaven of communion?

Surely it takes more than that to raise the dough. . . .

Prayer, trust.

Did you feel that you were an instrument?

I would have considered that pretentious. In my family, our upbringing was very severe in that respect.

Was prayer the most important resource for you?

Prayer is a vast, immense reality which is completely beyond me. My own words only enter into it as very poor prayer. And that is

TAIZÉ

as true now in my sixty-third year as it was when, at the age of twenty-five, I arrived in Taizé. It's true that the light of a presence can sometimes flash through our prayer, and there are no words to express that presence. Nevertheless, in the final analysis, prayer is always poverty-stricken.

So the yeast working in the dough, all that ecumenical evolution which had its starting-point in Taizé, has no rational explanation?

Absolutely none.

How do you evaluate the most important decisions of your life? The foundation of the community, for example?

Very soon, after I first arrived in Taizé, I knew that it would be possible to create a monastic 'order'. But I always refused to, right from the start. It would have been too unwieldy. A community, on the other hand, is able to adapt constantly to developments in human society, and society is developing more rapidly today than ever before. The most important thing is the sign-value of a community. Make it concrete. Over and over again this came up: make it concrete. Don't get lost in too many abstract ideas. This is where the farmer in me comes to the fore.

Didn't you ever regret the choice of Taizé as the site?

There was no definite choice of this place; there were other possibilities. Taizé, because of the situation at the time, provided the possibility of offering hospitality to political refugees. Otherwise, I have never been enthusiastic about this place.

What do you think today about your decision to study theology?

I never for one second considered theology a way of preparing for ministry in a parish. For me it was a means of becoming acquainted with contemporary Christian thought.

Then it was out of curiosity, in the wider sense of the term?

Perhaps out of necessity also, so as not to disturb my parents too much. My father was happy to see me enter on a course of studies which would last several years.

Your first years in Taizé must have been extremely difficult.

How could it have been otherwise? A situation of human isolation. The clash between nations at war. But I think I knew how to cope with my suffering. I would sing for hours at a time while I worked, and it seemed to me that joy could be found there: in singing a great deal, and praying three times a day.

You were never tempted to give up and leave it all?

Never. Not for one moment.

Humanly speaking, how is that possible?

I wonder too. I never thought about it.

Where did you find the strength to cultivate the land all alone and to take in refugees?

I said to myself: the more someone wants to live in response to the absolute of God's call, the more essential it is to insert that absolute into human suffering. To test the authenticity of a spiritual experience by confronting it with suffering humanity. When I was living alone with the political refugees, I had set up a small oratory in the house. I prayed there morning, noon, and evening, just as we do today. When some of the refugees wished to pray with me, I didn't want them to. I was afraid they might feel under an obligation, because I had shown them hospitality. I was afraid the hospitality had put pressure on their freedom of choice. I know

183

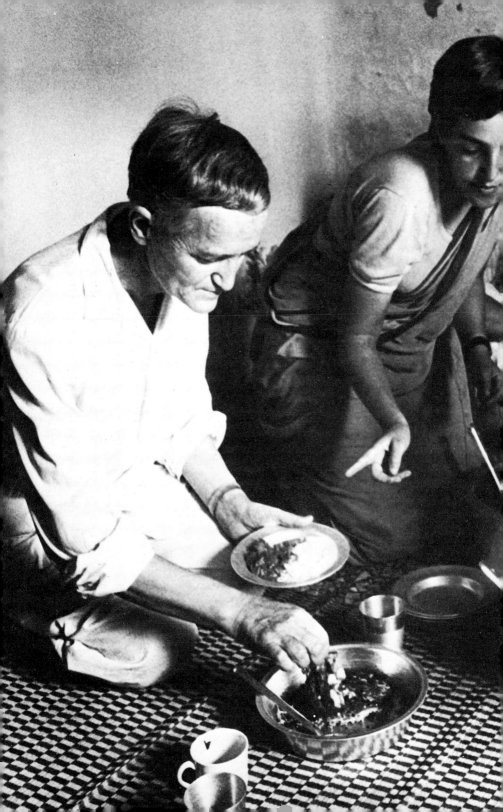

that one or two of them suffered from my refusal; they prayed in their rooms. I thought that if they felt bound to join me it wouldn't be honest, it wouldn't be fair. Those two words played a large role in the consciousness of my family.

Did you expect or hope that others would join you?

When I was still on my own, I wrote a little booklet to ask the question, to indicate that this was a possibility.

I have the impression that in later years Pope John XXIII had a special influence on you.

Shortly before Pope John's death, I had a very long audience with him. I was accompanied by two of my brothers. I asked the Pope: 'How do you see the future of Taizé? What do you expect of us?' And then Pope John said some words which, you might say, made us a part of the reality of the Church. I have never wanted to repeat those words, but I refer to them constantly myself.

What in particular attracted you to Pope John?

I had a meeting with him once a year. Through him I was able to understand all the dimensions of the Church which the mind of man does not even suspect. Pope John could have spoken to us in the language of tradition. But instead his words went so far, they were so powerful, that even today, at every difficult moment, they urge me on.

Sometimes I have the feeling that you have a greater natural affinity with the Catholic tradition than with the Reformed tradition in which you grew up.

It's true that the influence of my grandmother and the years I spent in a Catholic family helped to broaden my mind. But I am convinced that the Church is so much more extensive than we can imagine. We are far from having sounded its breadth, height, and depth. In this respect it's easy for me to accept the fact that there are different mentalities, even within my own community. My conscience would be uneasy if I forced someone to go along with a current which wasn't right for him.

In general we know the historical facts which led to the Council of Youth. But how do you explain the attraction you exercise over young people?

When I was young, I was surprised that young people were made to keep a certain distance from their elders. I respected that distance, I don't think I suffered from it, but it still astonished me. At that time when there were so many divisions among human beings, I kept asking myself: why these oppositions, these definitive judgements, this inability to understand one another? And I wondered: does there exist, here on earth, a way to understand everything in another person? Then came a day – I can still remember the date, and I could describe the place: the subdued light of a late summer evening, darkness settling over the countryside – a day when I made a resolution. I said to myself: if such a way exists, begin with yourself and commit yourself to understanding everything in every human being; become the man who can understand everything. That day, I knew that the resolve I had made was final and would last until I died. It consisted simply of returning again and again for the rest of my life to that once-and-for-all resolution: seek to understand instead of seeking to be understood. I think that it was then that I began to listen to young people. At the end of my theological studies, I was asked to be president of the Christian Student Federation at the university and also president of the students in the school of theology. It didn't interest me very much but I finally accepted. And that was an important step in discovering more and more how to understand young people in a still wider and greater way.

Do you mean that what attracts the young is your patience in listening to them?

No. But almost every evening, when I stay in our church listening to them, sometimes until two o'clock in the morning, I say to myself again and again: in my own youth, deep within myself, I would have wanted to be listened to the same way that I listen. Why are they suffering? What causes the knots within them? What are their inner prisons? And then immediately another question arises: what are each one's special gifts? That's the important thing. Everything else, the past, even the moment which has just gone by, is already drowned with Christ in the water of baptism.

What makes you love the young so much that you identify yourself with them? What is the secret of loving?

It's not just the young. I love the old, the very old, and children, and babies. I think the secret of loving came down to me directly from my great-grandmother, through my grandmother and my mother. They had that gift. On the day my mother died, at the age of ninety-three, she felt the need to say a few simple words to a young man she loved very much, who had lost his parents when he was still young. She could hardly utter them because of her difficulty in breathing, but she wanted to tell him that life was still going to be beautiful for him. And in her last hours, when I was beside her, she repeated the same words: don't worry, I'm going away but all is well.

What precisely are your feelings after you have spent hours at night talking privately with young people?

I say to myself: how is it that the heart becomes so large as it grows older? How is it that I love that poor girl who tells me how she has felt rejected throughout her life, then of her hope in a boy's love which has recently crumbled, a girl without physical beauty, with nothing to make her attractive? I ask myself: why do I love her, her or another? I have no answer. Even if man has his limitations, it seems as if the heart can grow to infinity. Luckily I am able to remember almost all they tell me. I pass from one to the other, often quickly, but I remember years later what they have told me. I forget the names, but I remember faces and words. For an instant, in that relationship, those young people find in me a brother, a father. And I fully accept the fact that they go away again and find a similar relationship elsewhere.

Did you inherit that?

When I was young, it was a convention not to listen much to others. In the name of human dignity, people didn't talk much about themselves. For my part, I said nothing about my difficulties to my parents; I didn't want to burden them. With the passing of time, by making use of my intuition, by reading, by conversing with able people, I became more sensitive. But I never felt specially called to the young. I never dreamed that one day at Taizé we would be experiencing such an influx of young people from so many countries, week after week.

In your opinion, what is the reason for that?

We have no method, no system. We have one passion: helping them to discover how to live creatively with the gifts they possess. Why do they imprison themselves in anguish over the past? Why is their past not already drowned in the water of baptism? What are their gifts? What causes their lack of trust in God, who is not interested in what is over and done with but only in what lies before us, the creation of a poem of love together with God, a poem which includes times of difficulty. Using one's discernment and intuition is part of 'understanding everything'. I ask God to keep me from making mistakes, from making too many errors of judgement in

189

my private conversations with so many young people. I ask him for the ability to be able to plunge into what the other cannot understand so as to reveal him to himself, to reveal to him the creative forces alive within him. To free others, it is essential for a communion to be created. If I wanted to liberate others without being first of all a man of prayer and communion, I would become a doctrinaire of liberation.

Sometimes people compare you with St Francis of Assisi. What do you think about that?

It's something which would never even occur to me. When people say exaggerated things to me, I change the subject. When I am thanked for the spirit of Taizé, I reply that there is no spirit of Taizé. Then some people ask me for autographs or other nonsense of that sort. I tell them that a Christian cannot agree with expressions focusing on himself and not on the one Reality that matters. I am a humble servant and I will remain so until my dying day.

Are there saints or contemporary Christians who are especially inspiring to you?

Among the witnesses to Christ, I esteem Saint Teresa of Avila most of all because of the fire within her, the way she totally gave her life, while at the same time retaining her realism and her ability to achieve concrete results. She combined the two dimensions, the practical and the spiritual, within herself. As for those whom I knew while they were still alive, Pope John XXIII is undoubtedly the one who affected me the most.

What does being prior mean to you?

During one of our community's council meetings, I reminded my brothers that I have always refused the name of prior inside the community. That word is for the outside world; it expresses a ministry. But for the community, I am only the servant of communion. I had noticed, especially while travelling, that the name of Prior of Taizé earned me some special consideration. To be shown such consideration because of a Church title is not in the spirit of the Gospel. And sometimes I state clearly why I reject what has so often wrought havoc in the Churches: the seeking of prestige and honour through ecclesiastical office.

*

Brother Roger, why do so many young people from all over the world come to Taizé? What attracts them?

I have no idea. I could list various reasons, of course. But what would they be worth? On 20 August 1940, when I arrived here alone on my bicycle, Taizé was a partly ruined village of fifty inhabitants, in the midst of a human wasteland. Today the hill of Taizé is like an oasis.

Do you think that the young are attracted by the life of the brothers – a life of community, struggle, and prayer?

For my brothers who have chosen the absolute of a vocation to community, there is no happy medium. My deepest desire is for everyone to understand that. That vocation always brings us closer to an invisible martyrdom: bearing in our own bodies the marks of Christ Jesus, so as to be a sign of God's radiance, a sign of the transcendence of his love. The result is God's joy, in all who go to the extreme of this vocation. In a life in community, just as in every vocation within the Church, the greatest temptation is to settle down, to find a comfortable corner.

Saint Paul calls the Church the Mystical Body of Christ, and he speaks of the different functions of its members. Which organ of the body, symbolizing what function, would you call Taizé?

Being a parable of communion open to the universal. A parable lived in the lives of brothers of different origins, Catholic and non-Catholic. Nothing but a parable to advance towards that unique communion called the Church. A number of times during our existence as a community, people have tried to talk us into starting a new Church. We could have done so, but such an undertaking would have contradicted our search for communion, our passion for the Church and for the ecumenical vocation. It would have made us part of that well-known process which in past centuries has fragmented the Body of Christ. We have suffered too much from that process to use it ourselves.

At a given moment the Council of Youth abolished its own cell-groups and communities all over the world, and suggested that everyone become instead part of what already exists. And yet Christ himself said that we should not put new wine into old wineskins.

By abolishing the small cell-groups which had sprung up and which sometimes were even labelled 'Taizé groups', by avoiding everything that could make the Council of Youth seem to be a movement, we are trying to remind one another that Taizé is only a small community. Everything that may arise from this community only exists as an offering to the universal communion of Christians. A community like ours is called above all to be yeast in the dough and to set working other raising agents, well mixed into the dough of the Church and of mankind.

A person awakens others to God above all by the life he leads. In the same way, a community awakens others to the meaning of communion and stimulates ferments of communion more by its life than by its words. Words only become credible when they are lived out. Words are necessary but they come afterwards, to express something that is already being lived out.

So you see Taizé, in the Body of Christ, as a member which would like to link up the other members?

Yes. And at the same time as a reference-point of friendship and understanding for many others who are not Christian. When you see Hindus and Muslims here, when you hear some of them speak of Christ as their brother, then you realize that the mystery of the Church is far vaster than you imagined. You are dumbfounded to discover that those people live an absolute of God with such intensity that we recognize ourselves in them.

Taizé lives at the point of intersection of all sorts of antitheses. I'm thinking, for example, of fundamentalism and liberalism, of pacifism and revolution, of pietism and humanism, etc. Isn't it difficult to reconcile these currents while at the same time maintaining a visible identity?

I'm not aware that we lie at the intersection of these different currents. I believe rather that an identity is given to anyone who chooses above all else to respond to the absolute of God and his Christ. That's all there is to it.

Yet you cannot deny that the young people who come here represent the great plurality which is the People of God. Aren't you afraid of the growing pluralism within the Church?

No, because it corresponds to the diversity of the human family. It would worry me if Christians mistook uniformity for communion.

But doesn't this pluralism carry with it the danger of ending up with no Christian identity at all?

An identity will remain to the extent that, in its heart of hearts, there remain places where the unanimity of the faith is expressed, the same descent towards the sources of the paschal mystery, the mystery of the Risen Christ.

How do you personally see Taizé's identity?

When you are on the inside of a reality, it's difficult to see its identity. It's true that, in this year of 1977, we have come closer than ever before to fullness. Within the community as well as among the multitudes of young people who visit our hill, a period of maturity has begun. After the shocks of birth, we are approaching what we hoped for most of all: a fullness of prayer and a passionate search for God which never forgets either the building of the city of man or solidarity with the unfortunates of this earth. On the contrary, this solidarity is being lived more intensely than ever, more concretely than in periods which were perhaps too idealistic. A few years ago, among some young people, there were more ideas about man and the transformation of society, but fewer concrete commitments, less real participation in human situations.

In that case, shouldn't the Churches listen more to what is happening here?

We are the ones who wish to listen. It's when we listen that things happen.

Shouldn't the Churches also listen more than they do?

Listen to the young in general, listen to what the Spirit is saying to the Churches through the young, yes, but not to Taizé in particular. There is no 'message of Taizé'.

Is the voice of the young heard in the Church?

Almost not at all, and it is a cause for despair among many. Very many young people have the impression, as they put it, that 'the Churches are only trying to take them over'. So they prefer to stay away. Personally I keep on telling them: be yeast in the dough,

196

don't run away, let's be yeast in the dough together, that's our community's vocation too.

At Taizé – as in most of the Churches in the Western world, to be sure – the number of visitors from the middle classes is far greater than the number of young people from the working class who come. Isn't that contrary to your ideal?

During the last three years, the number of workers who come to Taizé – blue-collar, white-collar, or agricultural workers – has been constantly on the increase. Naturally their presence depends on the holidays they have. Working people have less time off than university students. But there are times when working people represent more than a third of the total number of young people present.

Isn't that very little?

The tension towards universality which inspires us impels us to go as far as we personally can towards the world of the poorest, the most under-privileged, the most neglected, and share their lives. My brothers are doing this in several of our fraternities. Last year I myself spent a while in a Calcutta slum, and soon I will be going to Hong Kong to live for a short time in a poor district there. It's not easy, it requires effort, but it's essential for me not simply to let young people do this but to live there myself, to share the living conditions of the poorest.

Speaking of these slums, wouldn't it be consistent with the dynamic of the provisional to transport Taizé to Southern Asia or to Latin America?

We have only one house in the world, and that's the one in Taizé. And that house, incidentally, still looks too much like a nineteenth-century lady! We are doing all we can to remove the last signs of

that. I acquired this house in 1940, for very little, the price of a car. At the time there was also a bit of land, which cost about as much as another car, but we gave it to the agricultural co-operative set up in our village. We refuse to start foundations elsewhere. Today the Southern hemisphere no longer accepts such foundations from the North. In the Southern hemisphere, we can only live provisionally, a very few of us at a time. Two or three white faces, present in a slum of a country in the Southern hemisphere for a short while, is all that the world of the poor can accept at the moment.

Have your relationships with the various Protestant Churches changed fundamentally since the fifties?

In the fifties, some Protestant Church leaders could not accept the idea of life-long commitments. It was so contrary to more than four centuries of Reformation history. Today they understand and I think that, in general, we inspire their trust.

With regard to the Protestant Churches, I would like to say that the best they have to offer, their specific gift, is to be the Churches of the Word. They have been consistent throughout their history in their use of Scripture as an immediate source for living God in the midst of society. As soon as a word of God has been understood (not a word taken in isolation, of course, but always situated in Scripture as a whole), as soon as a word of God has been grasped, it has an impact on our personal life. It is important to put into practice immediately, no matter what the cost, that word, that little bit of Scripture that we personally have grasped.

If we remember the quality of some of the great Protestant divines of the seventeenth and eighteenth centuries, those whose writings and poems were turned by Bach, for example, into chorales and hymns of an intensity rarely achieved, we can understand better to what extent the Word of God was loved, taken seriously in personal life, how it stimulated a whole inner life, how it penetrated, disturbed, and transformed the Protestant Christian to the very depths of his being. Isn't that the best of Protestantism?

And how do you see the Catholic Church?

Pope John XXIII welcomed us so generously that he changed something in my life. Pope Paul has continued this. Such a welcome would have been unthinkable in the fifties.

The Catholic Church is above all the Church of the Eucharist, that is her specific gift. Of course the Catholic Church is also the Church of the Word, but she has enabled the Eucharist to be a focus of unanimity of the faith, like an underground stream flowing through her entire history. The unchanging presence of Christ in the Eucharist is always received in a childlike spirit, until the very evening of our lives. That is why when Pope Pius X, at the beginning of this century, opened the Eucharist to children, he displayed rare powers of intuition.

In living from the Eucharist, during long inner silences when it seems as if nothing is happening, many people have matured the great decisions of an entire lifetime, the new beginnings, setting out once more to live Christ with men. They let themselves be penetrated down to the very depths of their beings, down to what today we call the levels of the unconscious. It is then that, even when the heart senses nothing, the Eucharist brings to life that saying of Christ's: 'The Kingdom is within you'. And this is true even for someone who hardly dares hope for it.

The Eucharist is there for those who are starving for Christ. In consequence, when Christ calls, when a baptized person, one of God's poor, is hungry for the Eucharist and wishes to approach it in repentance of heart, how can we turn him away?

The Secretary General of the World Council of Churches, Dr Eugene Carson Blake, wrote in 1974 how much he appreciated 'your attempt to find a way out of the present impasses in ecumenism'. Do you feel you succeeded?

I wouldn't dare say so. Dr Eugene Carson Blake was both a humble man and a bold one. He was a man of the sources, a man of Scripture, a man of prayer. He had a daring vision which would have enabled him, had he had the means, to go very far. But with the courage that characterized him, he could only evoke fear. When he suddenly left office, I realized that the ecumenical institution was going to enter a period of crisis. During his last year in office he came to Taizé five times. I realized what it means for a man to go through the wilderness.

Some people refer to Taizé as a springtime in the Church.

Pope John was the one who used that expression first, one day as I was coming into his library.

Springtime brings flowers. What are Taizé's flowers?

We see many; they spring from overflowing hearts. They grow on humanity's wounds and on the wounds of the Church. A wound is like a place of darkness that Christ chooses as his dwelling – to live in us, to live in the Church, and starting from that spot to bring creative energies to birth. It is on those wounds that the flowers grow. They are all colours: some are dark and sombre, others brilliant.

When are they sombre and when brilliant?

They are sombre when they are one with the troubles of mankind, when they bloom despite misunderstandings. They are brilliant when they grow out of the incredible creativity possessed by so many women and men in the Church. Dark or bright, they all have the same scent: the scent of confident trust. Sometimes I ask myself where it comes from – this unfailing trust which unites us, young and old and, in my case, an older person of a certain age. The only answer: this trust is a kind of reflection of God's joy within us. The confidence shown in us, poor men living out in the country, is breathtaking. It is true that normally we are enveloped in trust.

The word 'trust' often comes up in our conversations. It seems to me that the heart of your struggle is a combat of trust against fear.

Not exactly. I am convinced that when a Christian finds himself in the dead-end of worry and fear, he has no other way out than trust. Last winter, when I held in my arms tiny Marie Sonaly, that four-and-a-half-months-old baby whose mother died giving birth, who was entrusted to me and whom I brought back to Taizé, I was worried that she would die. For weeks I carried that baby in my arms, for hours at a time. I even learned to write holding her in my arms. At those times she slept well. I said to myself: if she has only a few weeks to live, as long as she has begun to trust. . . . My anxiety would deny the love of God; if she dies I will have it out alone with God and it won't be easy, but as long as she lives, I want to be nothing but trust for that little child. And in the end she did live, she is with us at Taizé, she sings, everything is fine.

How can you learn to trust? How can you learn to be vulnerable?

We are all vulnerable, to a greater or lesser extent according to the period of life. It's not necessary to learn to be vulnerable, that's part of human nature. The wound in every human being, deeper in some than in others, especially the wounded innocence of our childhood, makes us all vulnerable beings. All through my life, especially when I was young, I have sung for hours, until I attained joy and serenity. Sometimes I have to sing soundlessly, so as not to disturb others.

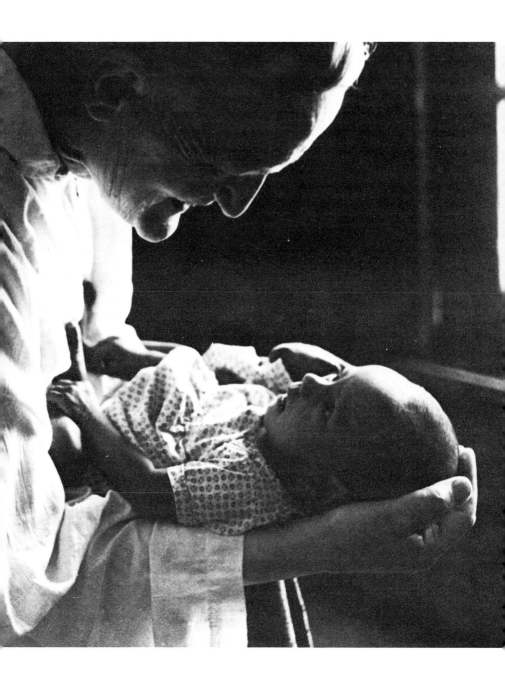

Have you learned this from the children you love to have around you?

When the children are beside me in church, I often look into their eyes. Through the simple words they say to me, I discover in those beings, who are still very intuitive and close to God, something of their anxiety and their wound. And then I love them more than ever.

How long will the Council of Youth last?

No one can set the date; no one knows.

At the opening of the Council of Youth, you spoke about crossing the desert.

That desert where we move from one oasis to the next. . . .

*

Brother Roger, what signs of hope do you see in the Church today?

All over the world, peoples and societies are being shaken. If the Church is an integral part of these societies, it is to be expected that she too will undergo the same shocks. But the present trials are opening new ways forward. Many older people in the Church, even very old people, have been made more transparent by the present trials and some of them have begun to listen to the younger generations.

Where do you see these new ways forward?

Everywhere tiny awakenings are taking place, small groups springing up. If these small communities place Gospel leaven in the dough of old parishes fearful of their future, then the hardened crust of those old parishes breaks apart. When these small groups, instead of running away, remain within, energies are liberated and

TAIZÉ

unsuspected creative forces come to life. Among the young there is a gift of communion with God and with men. They are over-turning the ramparts of old rigidities.

Can all this happen without suffering?

No, nothing happens without suffering, nothing happens outside of the paschal mystery. Our life is a continual re-living within our-selves of the paschal mystery – death and resurrection.

Do you also see dangers threatening the Church?

Self-sufficiency, denominational pride, parochialism, forming tiny Christian clubs that secrete insurmountable segregations. So many denominational organisms smother ferments of communion. As regards the separation of the Churches, nothing will change until once and for all they stop trying to decide who was right and who was wrong in their history, ancient and modern.

Can the Church become one day a place of communion, as long as church-goers remain an anonymous mass?

It is obvious that this state of anonymity destroys communion. But on the other hand, Christ spoke also to crowds. He had com-passion on the hungry multitudes. The faith of the simple, with all it contains which is inaccessible to small elites, is a pearl of great price. It finds expression, for example, in the great pilgrim-ages which are so popular in the Southern continents. This simple faith is not the faith of anonymous masses, but the burning and personal trust of humble men and women whose hearts are over-flowing with confidence. When my brothers and I have the oppor-tunity of taking part in such pilgrimages, we are struck by this trust shown by very poor people. If this simple faith is rejected, a vacuum is created which nothing else can fill. Such simple faith is often accompanied by a thirst for renewal, and the renewal is rapidly assimilated, since there was already a continuity of the presence of Christ. When a vacuum has been created, on the other hand, often out of purism and the inability to comprehend the treasures of the faith of common people, then nothing can grow, it's like a devastated countryside.

When the universal Church has expanded on such a large scale, isn't it necessary to find a smaller scale at a local level?

Of course. But not to the extent of seeing the Church subdivided to the point of atomization. Otherwise the vitality of the small groups causes the sense of universal solidarity to explode and disappear. Christian life is lived in the tension created by this dialectic.

Do you find that the Church takes enough of a stand regarding the gulf between the rich and the poor in the world?

The spur of Marxism awakened from their long slumber a great many Christians who had been sleeping for centuries, perhaps since the Middle Ages. Sharing spiritual goods creates a sort of illusion when it is separated from the sharing of material goods. If the Church began to set out courageously to live a parable of sharing, she could provide an answer. But sharing must be undertaken as an act of trust in God, not out of constraint.

Are you against a forced sharing of material possessions?

Yes. If people are pressured into sharing, that immediately creates doctrinaires of sharing. And every form of doctrinairism turns Christians into living dead.

How can the People of God free itself from its materialism?

When the Church becomes poorer and loses her confidence in the efficiency of great material resources, she is on the road to renewal and will take many others, believers and non-believers, along with her. In the Church the power of material resources inspires fear. A powerful man inspires fear and, although he may indeed call himself a Christian, he does not awaken others to life in God; his faith loses its credibility. The same is true of the Church.

Do you already see a way leading to renewal?

It lies in a transformation of the younger generations, who no longer accept the easy way out provided by material resources, people making careers for themselves in the Church, and all forms of 'going along with the herd'.

Do you believe that the Church can prevent the self-destruction threatening the world?

God is so bound up with mankind that wherever there is a human being, there is a reflection of God's image. When Christians and other believers become aware of this, they are capable of accomplishing a great deal to create a new consciousness within humanity. A communion among believers has become more essential than ever in the face of the threat of nuclear war. The younger generations are looking for a new way forward. At Taizé there are young Muslims, and young Hindus, who are determined to search together with young Christians. Peace on earth presupposes the encounter of all men of goodwill.

But in the meantime the arms race has reached the point of absurdity, and Christian politicians and statesmen have done nothing to oppose it.

For that reason, the vocation of a universal pastor in the Church is becoming essential. He could speak, implore, travel around, go to places where great dangers threaten, in the name of all human beings of goodwill, and be the spokesman for that part of humanity which considers such threats no longer acceptable.

Do you think you will see that unique universal pastor in your lifetime ?

I have seen him already, in John XXIII. And now, at the end of his life, Paul VI has within him a reflection of the holiness of God. During my last private audience with him, I sat opposite him as usual. My peasant origins made me need to support myself with my two elbows on his wooden desk. And I said to myself: the holiness of God resides in this man and he doesn't realize it, the burdens he bears are so heavy. At another audience I said to the Pope: God does not punish his Church, he cannot punish the Body of Christ; sometimes God leads us into the desert, sometimes he leaves us in a vast silence, but he does not punish. The Pope raised both his hands but said nothing.

Does the universality of this pastor depend more upon his personality than his office ?

As I said recently at the Italian Eucharistic Congress in Pescara, where I had been invited to speak, the office of universal pastor needs to be transfigured. Four and a half centuries ago, a part of Christendom fled from the Bishop of Rome. Today, many non-Catholic Christians are coming to realize how necessary it is not to flee but to stand with him and those around him, so that all who reside in the Vatican undergo a transfiguration and together become a community that is a witness to others, an image to be reflected everywhere else. Yes, by the simplest of means, offering hospitality, providing, in Vatican City, that small land of liberty, a welcome with the simplest of means, but a welcome as wide as the world. Needless to say, simple means do not imply an absence of communication across the globe. We all know how many persecuted Christians are sustained in their faith just by a voice broadcast over the radio waves of the Vatican. Such a 'witness community' will spark a parable of communion and will inevitably lead in its wake bishops and Church leaders, as well as Catholic and non-Catholic Christians all over the earth.

Many of the young wonder if such confidence is realistic, if an appeal of this kind will be listened to.

I think it will: perhaps the transfiguration has already begun. I see it with my own eyes when I meet certain men who have been made so transparent by suffering in the Vatican. But it's only a beginning.

Contrary to the world in which we live, the Bible doesn't seem to attach much importance to large numbers; it's always the few who pass on the torch.

Personally, I have always lived in the certainty that a small number of women and men, spread across the face of the earth, striving to reconcile in themselves struggle and contemplation, can change the course of history and reinvent the world. I spend my whole life repeating that.

What kind of people are able to live in that way?

Women and men of the sources, who know that nothing can separate them from Eternity's love, neither life nor death. They dare to take risks, to live dangerously, to come closer and closer to an invisible martyrdom.

Why do you say the martyrdom must be invisible?

Because it concerns no one else. What fascinates me in God is his humility. God doesn't impose himself. God is neither a dictator nor an army commander. He never forces our hand. God is so careful of human freedom that at times he is so silent that our hearts almost break. God made himself humble so as not to blind us by his overwhelming, infinite beauty, by a love which would overpower us. God gives all and asks nothing in return. That is why, for anyone who chooses the absolute of his call, there is no happy medium. Being women and men of communion means always coming closer to an invisible martyrdom, it means bearing in our bodies the marks of Jesus Christ. And that means becoming a sign of God's radiance, a sign of resurrection, a sign of the absolute of his love. It means continually becoming able to turn our lives into a poem of love with God.

If God is love, he is also vulnerability. Doesn't that frighten you?

Frighten is not the right word. An ancient prayer of the Church says that God's greatest power is the power to forgive. God is nothing but forgiveness and tenderness; he never condemns. Who can condemn us, when Jesus prays for us and in us?

A growing number of Christians believe we are approaching the Apocalypse.

I think that the Apocalypse occurs throughout human history, in successive stages. But that is all so far beyond us. We cannot manipulate people's fear of apocalyptic situations and so create a void, an abyss for them to fall into, a bad conscience in them. Winning followers for Christ in that way would be despicable. As early as the year 1000 there were people who announced the end of the world. In fact we know neither the day nor the hour. That shouldn't preoccupy us.

Will the Church rise with the Lord if she doesn't die with him?

The Church, if she wants to remain the Church, can only die to herself.

How?

By being the bearer of God's joy for every human being. Perhaps in that way she will come closer to an invisible martyrdom, but she shouldn't give any hint of it. That concerns only God and herself. Otherwise we would only end up with a doleful Church and doleful Christians. And then where could we find God's joy?

From the Author's Notebook

'No,' thunders the German with clenched fist, 'I'm no supporter of the terrorists. But I'm sick of the whole business in Bonn. It doesn't matter which side is in power, the Socialists are as bad as the Christian Democrats. And anyway, those so-called Christian Democrats should be forbidden to use the word "Christian" in their name. Is it Christian to play ball secretly with the oppressors in South Africa? Is it Christian to implement economic policies that cause the Third World to die of starvation? Is it Christian to put your welfare state, your "economic miracle", on a pedestal and worship it? God preserve me from that kind of Christianity!'

His opponent, another German, feels himself outclassed. He is not prepared for so much verbal violence. Somewhat timidly he asks his countryman a counter-question. How does he think conversion will come about? Will politics lead to conversion? 'Who's talking about conversion?' exclaims the first youth. 'When you sit down and analyse things, you know what's wrong. The rights of working people can only be won on the barricades!' And those of God only through the Lord Jesus, replies the other.

I wanted to spend a week in Taizé as part of a group of young people. And so here I am, sitting with a friend in a large tent amidst English people, Germans, Africans, a Greek, and someone from Lebanon. A heated discussion is in progress.

It became clear to me this week that the community attracts young people with quite a range of opinions. Among them are those who find in the Gospel the mandate to exercise political pressure and by so doing change the world for the better; those who look for salvation uniquely from a proclamation of the Word which will lead to personal conversion; those who try to combine the two; those who don't expect much from either; and those who are searching for a vision to guide them. I suspect that most people belong to the last category.

What do all those people find in Taizé? How are they rewarded? In what are they discouraged? To what extent are they helped to go further? Those questions have kept me busy the whole week. The brothers may well claim that there is no 'Taizé theology', that they have no specific message of their own, but a reality like the Council of Youth cannot avoid emphasizing certain things, placing recognizable markers in the stormy sea of ideological turmoil. What do those markers look like? What colour are they?

The answer to that question, it seems to me, can be found above all in the way in which Taizé connects the essential elements of the Christian message. Prayer, proclaiming the Word, community, micro-ethics (the traditional 'good works'), and social responsibility are all part of the Christian tradition. But it can hardly be denied that throughout the ages first this, then that element has been pulled out of context and made into an absolute. For every element you can find a time when it began to lead a whole life of its own. In today's Church the elements continue to co-exist, but for the most part they are not integrated with one another. Religious pluralism today is not a matter of one integral Christian message which is experienced and expressed differently in different cultures, but rather a loose collection of ideas about how that message should be lived out in the life of the individual. All the elements are there somewhere, but they are not linked to one another in any organic way.

In Taizé I have the impression that the connections are not just reaffirmed and emphasized, but that they are shown to be chemical in nature. Prayer, Bible reading, and micro-ethics really come into their own when practised in community. Community, in turn, gets its force and cohesiveness from Bible readings and prayer. Prayer and micro-ethics follow naturally from one another. And social responsibility, as expressed for example in political activity, seems to be a by-product of community in the widest sense. One element is thus supported by another and functions best in the presence of another.

Naturally this doesn't mean that one person can't be mainly concerned with politics, another with prayer, community, or taking care of the elderly. Within the Mystical Body of Christ each person has his own gifts and together they enable the whole to function. But that implies respect for the other's gifts, and never considering one's own function absolute. And always becoming existentially involved oneself. 'We *do* protest when we hear that people in certain countries are oppressed or exploited,' a brother told me today. 'But we are even more ready to go and live in such a country and share the lot of the persecuted. That's our protest.'

Such an attitude seems to me essentially different from the notion that social analysis *alone* or the proclamation of the Word *alone* must be the Church's response to the challenges of our time. Of course social analysis *too*, proclaiming the Word *too*. But as a means to total liberation. Otherwise liberation is indeed, in the words of Jorge, the boy from Argentina mentioned in the second chapter, 'an empty and meaningless word'.

Taizé is a good place to learn a new way of using our powers of perception. Not just because here people are so often together in silence, which inevitably cleans out the channels of the mind. Probably even more because of the cosmic dimension which is reflected in the landscape and which penetrates the liturgy in the Church of Reconciliation. 'Darkness is not darkness in your sight; night shines as bright as day.' I have seldom seen a sky as full of stars as here. And I have seldom felt so much a part of a cosmic company.

This cosmic dimension in the liturgy, of course, does not date from today or even yesterday. It is a treasure of the universal Church. But Taizé has not hesitated to search through the entire liturgical tradition and to take from it what seems meaningful for our time. And so in the Church of Reconciliation we are linked to the millions of believers who tried before us in prayer to follow in Christ's footsteps. This communion with the Christians of ages past is an important part of the picture which the Bible paints of the company of believers, and Taizé has inscribed it, so to speak, on its liturgical banner. Here I not only know I am a part of that company – I see it, hear it, and feel it. In the Psalms and the hymns we affirm our bond with the Father, with one another, and with all who have gone before us. In the intercessions we remember those among us who are suffering or who have been wounded in the front lines of the struggle. For me what is happening here has an all-embracing, cosmic significance.

In this too I feel that the community's history has played a part. Isn't it out of and through its history that Taizé's liturgy has grown? Isn't it above all on account of the growing pluralism of the community that new elements are constantly being added to its liturgy, first from one tradition, then another?

I am still wrestling with the question why this liturgy attracts so many young people. Basically it is traditional, and all over the world traditional forms are being discarded. Could this phenomenon have to do with the new meaning which can be discovered in old words? Perhaps it is true that new words in themselves do not always lead to a renewed and living image of God. Old words, on the other hand, can create an alienation which can only be overcome if you are prepared to take a new look at the realities hiding behind the words. I think this is what happens in Taizé, and it explains in part the attraction of its liturgy. The liturgy here is indeed related to day-to-day reality, to the society we all live in. This is possible, too, because here everything is regarded as provisional. When the church becomes too small a wall is torn down, and when a text becomes outdated it is either rewritten or mercilessly thrown on the garbage heap. Taizé does not collect family photos; it is always on the move, always concerned with the challenge of the day, or better still the hour. For how long? For quite a while yet, it seems to me, considering the brothers' average age. Age isn't always the important thing, though; Brother Roger is living proof of that. He will be on the move until he has gone home for good.

Community, as an essential part of what it means to be human, seems to break through the crust of the un and sub-conscious in Taizé. In nearly every conversation there are at least some people who really try to penetrate to the other's heart. I constantly get the impression that people speak more freely here than at home. Maybe it is because after a week most of them will never see each other again, although it is also because here spiritual community is nourished by various forms of physical community. We eat, sleep, walk, pray, and sing together, and all this makes it easier for us to stretch out our spiritual tentacles. Of course this life together is not without a touch of romanticism. But in a Church where the desires of the heart seem to be fulfilled less and less, this hardly calls for an apology.

There is a still deeper reason for this expanding communion on the hill here in Burgundy. It struck me as I was walking by the old country house in which the brothers live. Behind those walls live some eighty men who, in order to be together, have had to clear practically all the hurdles that history could set up. First, in the Reformation tradition, the thorny barriers of scepticism regarding the monastic life. Then the obstacles separating the different Protestant denominations to which the brothers belong. Then the centuries-old, almost unbridgeable gap between Protestantism and Catholicism. And on top of all that, the barbed wire fences that have estranged the Western Church in particular from exploited, oppressed young people. The family of brothers in Taizé has been able to create bonds with and among all these categories of people because, to begin with, they have taken all the above-mentioned barriers into their own home. About eighty brothers of different skin colour, nationality, age, background, denomination, and political leaning – and yet one and the same family, who share what they have, spiritually as well as materially.

Brother Roger told me that some time ago he had been advised to start his own Church. That he did not do so is fully consistent with the evolution described in these pages. Anyone seeking so single-mindedly for communion, anyone inspired to such an extent by the parable of the mustard seed, can and will function only within that unique communion called the Church. Whoever loses his life will find it. Taizé does not exist for Taizé. If it goes under and disappears into the universal Church, so what? As long as, in so doing, some yeast has been added to the worldwide dough of that Church. That's all that counts.

The very least that can be said of Taizé is that it has lit a clearly visible candle, a light to kindle other lights. And that is something, in a world where all roads seem to come to an end at one time or another in the darkness of meaninglessness, suffering, and death. Its light shines in the Church, where it goes beyond criticism to illuminate new inspirations and hesitant initiatives which sooner or later will lead to an authentic rebirth. It shines in the world, too, where Taizé ranges itself at the side of the needy, the oppressed, and the lonely, because it knows that in them Christ speaks to us, and that through them he will inherit the earth. Finally, its light shines personally on each of Taizé's many visitors, the tens of thousands of young people especially who lay their problems at the brothers' and at each other's feet. They fix their attention above all on the light within each one of them, the light they can either extinguish or fan into flame, the light which is called to take its place in the sea of light that will conquer the world. Each of them, says Taizé, can be a sign of hope. Together we can reinvent the world.

The embodiment of that hope is a small, greying man whose smile has a touch of sadness in it. More than anyone else, he has the right to express that hope: out of his hope, his trust, his love, there has come into being in the Church a movement of hope, trust, and love, which in the final analysis can only be compared with the new life that a Benedict or a Francis gave to the Church. Anyone familiar with its history knows that it has passed through

many an icy winter. But these winters are inevitably followed by new springtimes, when the sun of hope shines again and when new life blossoms forth. Taizé stands under the sign of such a springtime. In the place where young Roger Schutz, all alone, dug up the hard earth, communion is now being sowed; where he healed the wounds of refugees, the seed of struggle is now dying in the ground; and where he descended in contemplation into the solitude of his heart, there now blossoms the prayers of people who come from the four corners of the earth.

This place has captured my heart. I can only write about it in the language of love. As a sonnet to the Spirit, stammering, in self-surrender.

Prayer
   silence in.. p 85, 91
   priority of . p 85
   emotional + contemplative p 88
   teaches dependence p 92
is waiting p 158
   leads us to our neighbor p 158

Liturgy
  - described (Taizé) p 95, 96 f.

Church
  - needs to be visibly poor p 109

Contemplation   p 101 p 109

Silence is a mirror   p 103

Community
  - a frame of mind p 128

Violence - p 164